Cambridge Elements ≡

Elements in Cognitive Linguistics
edited by
Sarah Duffy
Northumbria University
Nick Riches
Newcastle University

METAPHOR, METONYMY, THE BODY AND THE ENVIRONMENT

An Exploration of the Factors That Shape Emotion–Colour Associations and Their Variation across Cultures

Jeannette Littlemore
University of Birmingham

Marianna Bolognesi
University of Bologna

Nina Julich-Warpakowski
University of Erfurt

Chung-hong Danny Leung
Hong Kong Metropolitan University

Paula Pérez Sobrino
University of La Rioja

CAMBRIDGE
UNIVERSITY PRESS

CAMBRIDGE
UNIVERSITY PRESS

Shaftesbury Road, Cambridge CB2 8EA, United Kingdom

One Liberty Plaza, 20th Floor, New York, NY 10006, USA

477 Williamstown Road, Port Melbourne, VIC 3207, Australia

314–321, 3rd Floor, Plot 3, Splendor Forum, Jasola District Centre, New Delhi – 110025, India

103 Penang Road, #05–06/07, Visioncrest Commercial, Singapore 238467

Cambridge University Press is part of Cambridge University Press & Assessment, a department of the University of Cambridge.

We share the University's mission to contribute to society through the pursuit of education, learning and research at the highest international levels of excellence.

www.cambridge.org
Information on this title: www.cambridge.org/9781009045582

DOI: 10.1017/9781009042468

First published 2023

A catalogue record for this publication is available from the British Library.

ISBN 978-1-009-04558-2 Paperback
ISSN 2633-3325 (online)
ISSN 2633-3317 (print)

Additional resources for this publication at www.cambridge.org/Littlemore

Cambridge University Press & Assessment has no responsibility for the persistence or accuracy of URLs for external or third-party internet websites referred to in this publication and does not guarantee that any content on such websites is, or will remain, accurate or appropriate.

Metaphor, Metonymy, the Body and the Environment

An Exploration of the Factors That Shape Emotion–Colour Associations and Their Variation across Cultures

Elements in Cognitive Linguistics

DOI: 10.1017/9781009042468
First published online: June 2023

Jeannette Littlemore
University of Birmingham

Marianna Bolognesi
University of Bologna

Nina Julich-Warpakowski
University of Erfurt

Chung-hong Danny Leung
Hong Kong Metropolitan University

Paula Perez Sobrino
University of La Rioja

Author for correspondence: Jeannette Littlemore, j.m.littlemore@bham.ac.uk

Abstract: By exploring the associations that people make between emotions and colours, looking at how they vary across languages, and exploring the explanations that people provide for the associations that they make, this Element provides insight into the ways in which humans express emotions through colour, and the reasons why they do so. Metaphoric (and metonymic) language and thought play a key role on several levels in the formation of emotion–colour associations, interacting with physical, environmental and social factors. A strong metaphorical connection between the valence of the emotion and the lightness of the colours with which it is associated, and between the intensity of an emotion and the saturation level of the colours with which it is associated is found. However, the strength of this association varies according to the linguistic background of the speaker, and the gender in which the emotion is presented.

Keywords: emotion, colour, language, culture, metaphor

ISBNs: 9781009045582 (PB), 9781009042468 (OC)
ISSNs: 2633-3325 (online), 2633-3317 (print)

Contents

1 What Are Emotions and Why Do We Associate Them with Colours?

1.1 Introduction

Humans have a complex, emotional relationship with colour. Although colour is basically visible light, and the different colours that humans perceive are simply the brain's response to different wavelengths and intensities of light, colours are inextricably linked with our emotions. Colours can alter our mood; muted colours can exert a calming effect while vibrant colours can cheer us up or make us feel excited. We use colour to obtain important information about our environment; colours can warn us off eating certain foods or touching certain plants, and when we are driving, they can tell us whether it is safe to cross a junction. We also express ourselves through colour, through the clothes we wear, the way we decorate our houses, and the colours that we choose when purchasing objects. It is therefore unsurprising that one of the key uses that we make of colour is in the expression and description of emotions. One of the aims of this Element is to explore why this is, and to investigate the roles played by metaphor, metonymy, the body and the environment in this respect. We are also interested in how and why emotion–colour associations vary across cultures.

Some of the associations that people form between emotions and colours are well entrenched (Sandford, 2014). For example, for many people, at least in the Western world, anger is associated with the colour red, calmness is associated with the colours 'blue' and 'green', and happiness is associated with the colour yellow (see, for example, Clarke & Costall, 2008; Kaya & Epps, 2004). Emotions have also been found to 'group together' in terms of the types of colours that they attract. A clear manifestation of this phenomenon can be found in a study conducted by Sutton and Altarriba (2016). They invited 170 English-speaking adults to write down the colours that they associated with randomly presented words, of which 29 referred to positive emotions (e.g. 'happy'), 35 referred to negative emotions (e.g. 'sad'), 41 referred to positive emotion-laden concepts (e.g. 'gift') and 55 referred to negative emotion-laden concepts (e.g. 'criminal'). They found that negative emotion words and negative emotion-laden words were most often likely to elicit a 'red' response, a finding that they point out is in line with previous research showing that red carries a negative meaning and is often associated with danger (Kuhbandner & Pekrun, 2013). They also found that words referring to negative emotions tended to be associated with the colour black, which they argue is consistent with the research showing that dark colours tend to be related to negative entities (Meier et al., 2007).

However, despite the presence of a limited number of 'well attested' emotion–colour associations, and the tendency for certain groups of emotions to attract certain groups of colours, there is considerable variation in the levels of consistency that are exhibited by different emotion–colour associations. This issue was investigated in depth in a two-part study by Fugate and Franco (2019). In the first part of their study, they showed seventy-four English-speaking adults ten emotions and asked them to select up to three colours that they associated with each emotion, and to indicate the strength of the association. The twenty-three colours used in the study were presented in the form of coloured patches (to rule out the effect of using the name of the colour). In the second part of the study, they worked with a larger participant pool (N = 104) and included a wider set of emotions and colours. In the first part of their study, they found that only four of the ten emotions surveyed (anger, fear, happiness and sadness) displayed statistically significant levels of consistency across participants in terms of the colours with which they were associated. The levels of consistency in the second part of the study were even lower. Fugate and Franco suggest that the lack of consistency found in their study may be indicative of the socially constructed and culturally based nature of emotion–colour associations. They also suggest that 'strong' associations that have been observed in previous studies may be due to the fact that participants were offered only a limited selection of colours from which to choose so they may have been forced into making an artificial choice.

Differences between emotions in their tendency to remain 'loyal' to a particular colour have also been found by Jonauskaite and colleagues (2020) in their study of emotion–colour associations made by 132 French-speaking adults. They asked participants to associate ten different emotions with colour labels and colour patches. They found that some associations were very frequent in their data (e.g. red-anger, red-love, yellow-joy), some occurred somewhat less frequently (e.g. blue-sadness), and others were rare (e.g. blue-love). They found that some colours were associated with a single specific emotion (e.g. white-relief), while others were associated with several specific emotions (e.g. red-love, red-anger; yellow-joy, yellow-amusement). They also found that other emotion–colour associations could be described in terms of emotion 'dimensions'. For example, the colour black was associated with mainly negative emotions, grey with negative and weak emotions, blue with positive emotions and green with positive and powerful emotions, a finding that chimes with Sutton and Altarriba's (2016) finding, which we mentioned earlier.

In this Element, we explore the associations that participants from six different linguistic backgrounds form between emotions and colours, and the explanations that they provide for these associations. We then analyse these explanations through a theoretical framework that draws on metaphor theory. Our study is underpinned by the key cognitive linguistic principle that emotion–colour associations, like many other form-meaning pairings are, to a large extent motivated. Like Sandford (2014), we suggest that they are conceptualised through 'metaphors and metonyms' that have their roots in embodied physical and psychological experiences. Through our study, we aim to provide a deeper understanding of the ways in which emotion–colour associations are established through these mechanisms, and to identify why emotion–colour associations vary so much in terms of their strength and their cross-cultural reach.

1.2 What Are Emotions?

To better understand why it is that people experience such strong relationships between emotions and colours, it is useful to take a step back and to consider a more fundamental two-part question: What exactly are emotions, and why do people feel the need to express them through the use of colours? Emotions involve physiological, cognitive and behavioural components, and different theories of emotions place differential emphasis on each of these components. Early theories of emotion such as the 'James–Lange' theory of emotion, which was developed in the nineteenth century (Cannon, 1927), suggested that emotions are almost entirely based on physiological arousal. For example, when one encounters a frightening scene, one's heart rate may increase, which leads to the emotion of 'fear'. Since then, a large number of psychologists working in the field of emotion have pointed out that physiological responses are insufficiently varied to account for the full range of emotions that people report (Barrett, 2017a,b; Lange et al., 1993; Schachter & Singer, 1962). More recent views of emotion suggest that the physiological response co-occurs with recognition at a cognitive level that one feels an emotion (such as fear), and that it is this co-occurrence which leads people to associate the two. Under this view, it is the context, rather than the physiological response alone, that leads one to recognise and experience emotion. Although stronger physiological responses tend to be linked to stronger emotions, people's previous experiences lead them to interpret the same physiological responses as different kinds of emotion. So, for example, the same increased heartbeat that one may experience in response to finding themselves on a high diving board may be interpreted by some as fear and by others as excitement.

In a pioneering study on the dimensions of emotion, Russell (1980) challenged the classic experimental paradigm in affective neuroscience that claimed that emotions can be classified into discrete and independent categories, each associated with specific neural structures. Based on clinical observations suggesting that people find it difficult to assess, discern and describe their own emotions, Russell proposed a bidimensional model, known as the 'circumplex model of affect', in which all affective states arise as products of not one, but two independent neurophysiological systems, one related to valence (a pleasure–displeasure continuum) and the other to arousal, or alertness. Russell and Barrett (1999) subsequently drew a distinction between 'emotional episodes' (which refer to what most people would understand by the term 'emotion': anger, fear, joy, surprise and so on) and 'core affect', which they describe as 'the most elementary consciously accessible affective feelings … that need not be directed at anything' (p. 806). They argue that 'core affect' involves just two dimensions: the degree of pleasantness and the degree of activation, which combine to shape a person's mood. Core affect fluctuates over time and involves one's general sense of pleasure or displeasure and tension or relaxation, depression or elation. Whereas core affect is relatively easy to describe and measure, emotional episodes are much more complex as they refer to types of human behaviour. As well as involving core affect, emotional episodes also involve a combination of overt responses to an object or stimulus, attention toward and appraisal of the object or stimulus, the experience of having the emotion and the physical effects of the experience. As such, they are much more difficult to describe. More recent work on emotions (Barrett, 2017b) suggests that the labels we give to emotional episodes, and thus the ways in which those episodes are understood, are to a large extent socially constructed. Our emotional responses to sensory stimuli and to other experiences are largely shaped by our previous experiences, and by societal expectations of the sorts of things that we are 'supposed to' feel in certain circumstances.

1.3 How and Why Do We Associate Emotions with Colours? The Role of Metaphor

Because of their complexity, it is very difficult to describe the qualitative aspects of emotional episodes directly, and even the labels that they are given can be used to express a wide variety of experiences. For example, the term 'anger' can be used to describe both a hot-headed outburst and a more continuous sense of underlying cold seething sentiment. Notice that in this example, we have made use of metaphor (where something is described in terms of its similarity to an unrelated entity) to describe two different experiences of anger, describing one as 'hot' and the other as 'cold'. Indeed, it has been shown that anger is often talked about metaphorically in terms of heat

(Kövecses, 2003, 2008; Lakoff & Johnson, 1980). Other metaphors that are commonly used to describe emotion involve spatial orientation, which is often used to describe happiness and sadness (happy is 'up', sad is 'down'), and pressure, which is used to describe the intensity of an emotion and the level of control that one has over one's emotions ('letting off steam', 'blowing up with anger'). The fact that metaphors allow us to describe abstract experiences in more concrete, tangible and physical terms makes them well-suited to communicating complex phenomenological experiences (Colston & Gibbs, 2021). For this reason, metaphorical language has been shown to be particularly prevalent when people attempt to describe emotional episodes (Kövecses, 2008; Ortony & Fainsilber, 1987).

Metaphor, and its close relation, metonymy (where something is described through reference to a related entity – Littlemore, 2015) also appears to play a role in the associations that people form between emotions and colours. In many cases, metaphor and metonymy appear to work together to establish associations between emotions and colours. If we take, for example, the association between anger and the colour red, it could be argued that the association has a metonymic origin involving a cause/effect relationship; the physical effect of anger (going red) is used to refer to the emotion of anger itself. However, the association goes beyond metonymy and shades into metaphor because certain qualities can be transferred from the colour to the emotion. For example, one might interpret the degree of redness (in terms of saturation) as a more intense state of anger, thus establishing a metaphorical connection between similar (gradable) structural properties of the colour (red) and the emotion (anger). Indeed, some emotion–colour associations involve broader metaphorical associations between colours and the emotions. For example, as we will see in Section 1.4, there is evidence to suggest that more positive emotions are represented by lighter colours and that more intense emotions are represented by more strongly saturated colours. The fact that metaphor and metonymy play a role in shaping the ways in which colours are used to describe and refer to emotion is perhaps to be expected, as these mechanisms have been shown to play a key role in shaping the meanings that people attach to colours more generally (Sandford, 2021).

The associations that are formed between emotions and colours are neither purely metaphorical nor purely metonymic. They are not purely metaphorical, as there is no overt comparison. Anger cannot be said to be 'like' red in the way that, for example, one might say that life is 'like' a journey. The fact that intensity and valence can be mapped onto saturation and lightness means that they are not purely metonymic either. The kinds of examples of metonymy that are normally cited in the literature on metonymy (which Littlemore (2015) terms 'prototypical' metonyms), such as the use of the term 'The White House' to refer to the US Government, or the use of the term '9/11' to refer to the events that took place on that date in New York, do not involve the kinds of direct mappings or correspondences that we find in emotion–colour associations. One might therefore describe the associations that people form between emotions and colours as 'metaphtonymic', as they involve elements of both metaphor and metonymy (Goossens, 1990; Ruiz de Mendoza & Díez, 2002; Ruiz de Mendoza & Galera, 2011).

Indirect evidence of the role played by metaphor and metonymy in the formation of emotion–colour associations can be found in explanations offered by participants for the associations that they form. For example, Clarke and Costall (2008) conducted a qualitative investigation in which they asked sixteen English-speaking participants to describe the emotions that they associated with eleven key colour terms, and to provide reasons for those associations. They found that the participants associated orange, yellow and red with what they termed 'active' emotions; participants reported the colour red to be a highly emotive colour and associated it with emotions such as love, anger and passion, whereas orange and yellow were more likely to be associated with warmth, happiness and cheerfulness. In contrast, the colours green and blue were more likely to be associated with what Clarke and Costall termed 'passive emotions' that are associated with low anxiety levels; these colours were more likely to be described as sad, calm or peaceful. Clarke and Costall also found relationships between valence and lightness: light colours were more likely to be associated with positive emotions and dark colours were more likely to be associated with negative emotions. These relationships were referred to explicitly by partici-pants, with one of the participants claiming that 'light colours are always happy regardless of the colour' (408). There were also indirect references to a per-ceived relationship between saturation (i.e. the intensity of the colour as deter-mined by the absence of greyness) and emotional intensity; for example, the colour grey, which is low in saturation, was widely reported to be associated with a lack of emotion. Some of the justifications that the participants provided for their choices referred to cultural practices, such as the fact that people wear black for funerals. Other answers appeared to involve personification of the colours themselves, with one participant commenting that 'orange is a more relaxed type of happy', and that 'yellow is a more bouncy happy colour' (p. 409). These findings illustrate the range of factors that are at play when people discuss the associations that they perceive between emotions and colours.

Many of the metonymic associations that people make between emotions and colours appear to be based on bodily experiences. For example, when we are angry, we may go red in the face, and this metonymic cause–effect relationship appears to motivate the association that many people make between the emotion anger and the colour red. Other metonymic associations appear to be shaped by the ways in which we interact with our environment. For instance, when the sun comes out, we feel more cheerful, which may partly explain why yellow, the colour typically associated with sunlight, is a 'cheerful' colour. Equally, being by the sea can make us feel calm and relaxed, which may partly explain why blue is a 'calm' colour, and green's calming effects may be due to its generic associations with nature and plants, which people often perceive as relaxing. Again, the associations appear to involve a metonymic cause–effect relationship.

The strength of the metonymic, environmentally based associations that people form between colours and emotions has been found to be affected by where people live. Jonauskaite and colleagues (2019a) investigated the associations between yellow and joy that were made by 6,625 participants from fifty-five countries and explored the ways in which they varied according to geographical, climate-related and seasonal factors. They found that participants who live further away from the equator and in rainier countries are more likely to associate yellow with joy, perhaps reflecting the fact that the rarity of sunshine in such countries makes the people who live there value it more, as they are less likely to associate it with drought. These findings suggest that the natural physical environment plays an important role in shaping the emotions that people associated with different colours. There are however some emotion–colour associations that are more difficult to explain in physical or environmental terms. It is not clear, for example, why envy and jealousy are associated with the colour green in English while they are associated with yellow in German, or why the colour red is associated with happiness in many East Asian languages. These associations appear to be more culturally based, and to some they may appear arbitrary.

In related work, Soriano and Valenzuela (2009) suggest four possible explanations for why associations between emotions and colours arise. Their first explanation is that the associations reflect the physiology of emotional experience. For example, as previously mentioned, red might be associated with anger because we go red in the face when we are angry. Their second explanation is what they term 'metaphor'. By metaphor, they mean broadly 'primary metaphor': the basic connections that exist between abstract experiences, such as 'good' and 'bad' and concrete environmental experiences such as 'light' and 'dark', and which are thought to develop partly as a result of real-world experiences, such as the fact that one may feel happier on sunny days (e.g. Grady, 1997; Sandford, 2021). They discuss the conceptual association between lightness and valence, and they report some of the extensive research findings showing that light colours automatically elicit a positive evaluation of objects whereas dark colours automatically elicit negative evaluations (Meier & Robinson, 2005; Meier et al., 2007). The third explanation that they propose relates to the fact that colours themselves have the ability to elicit emotional reactions. For example, exposure to the colour red has been found to enhance one's sense of alertness and urgency, which appears to have a strong metonymic basis. The fourth explanation that they offer is that both colour words and emotional words share similar connotative structures. They suggest that the emotional meanings of colours emanate from the situations or objects in real life where that colour is present. These could be naturally occurring entities, such as the red colour of blood, the green colour of grass or the blue colour of the sky, or cultural artefacts such as the fact that people wear black for funerals, red lights signal the need to stop and red signs alert us to danger, or that baby girls may be dressed in pink. In support of this last hypothesis, they report findings from an Implicit Association Test conducted with 115 adult Spanish speakers, which showed that people form unconscious associations between the colours red, blue, yellow and green, and different levels of evaluation, potency and activity.[1] Again, metonymy appears to play a role in the establishment of these associations. The natural world makes use of red and yellow to advertise threats such as poisonous creatures that should be avoided (Wee & Gopalakrishnakone, 1990), and these colours are often used to signal danger in warning and hazard signs. As humans are diurnal creatures, who are awake in the daytime and who sleep at night, the colour of a blue sky signals to the brain that it is daytime and that we should be awake (Wahl et al., 2019). Although these explanations have a deep experiential basis, in that they are bodily based or emerge from the interaction with the near environment, many of the associations that people form between emotions and colours appear to be more language- or culture-specific (Kövecses, 2005). For example, when asked to talk about associations between colours and emotions, participants often refer to linguistic expressions (e.g. 'seeing red' or 'feeling blue') which suggests that the linguistic background may play an important role in forming the associations (Fetterman, Robinson & Meier, 2012).

With the exception of Clarke and Costall's (2008) small-scale study, which was mentioned earlier, no studies to date have explored in detail and at scale the explanations that people offer for the associations that they make between emotions and colours. Furthermore, no large-scale studies to date have looked at how these explanations vary across cultures, and no studies have analysed the

---

[1] 'Evaluation' and 'activity' are Osgood, Suci, and Tannenbaum's (1957) original terms for what we now refer to as 'valence' and 'arousal'. 'Potency' refers to 'strength'.

roles played by metaphor and metonymy in the establishment of the associations. Investigating the explanations that people provide for these associations may help to provide deeper insights into the ways in which emotional experiences, as expressed through colour associations, vary across individuals, and the extent to which this variation relates to people's experiences of their own bodies and the linguistic, physical and cultural environments in which they live. By focusing on the reasons that people provide for the associations that they form, we hope to develop a deeper understanding of the relationship between people's inner and outer worlds.

In this Element, we report findings from an investigation into the associations that are made between emotions and colours by people from different linguistic/cultural backgrounds, and the explanations that are offered by the participants who have made the associations. We look at the extent to which the valence of the emotion relates to the lightness of the colours with which it is associated and the extent to which the intensity of the emotion relates to the degree of saturation of those colours. We also explore how these factors vary according to the linguistic/cultural background of the participants, and look at the reasons behind people's choices.

In the remaining parts of this section, we explore the various factors that account for the associations that people form between emotions and colours, and consider the extent to which these associations are shared by participants from different linguistic backgrounds. From these discussions, we then draw up a list of research questions that form the basis of our study.

1.4 Cross-Linguistic and Cross-Cultural Variation in Emotion–Colour Associations

As mentioned in Section 1.3 associations between emotions and colours have been shown to vary across languages and cultures, but there are some similarities. For instance, associations between the colour red and anger have been found in English (Waggoner & Palermo, 1989), Hungarian (Kövecses, 2005), Chinese (Chen et al., 2016), Japanese (Hanada, 2018; Matsuki, 1995) and Polish (Mikolajczuk, 1998). In contrast, significant variation has been found with respect to the emotions that people associate with the colour blue. In the United States, blue is associated primarily with sadness, whereas in France it is also associated with anger or fear (Barchard et al., 2017). Associations that people make with the colours white and yellow are also susceptible to significant cross-linguistic and cross-cultural variation. In the West, the colour white is primarily associated with purity, and yellow is sometimes associated with hatred, while in China, these colours are associated with righteousness and trustworthiness (Fadzil, Omar & Murad, 2011).

Linguistic and cultural influences interact in complex ways to shape emotion–colour associations. Many emotion–colour associations operate outside the realm of language, and manifest in non-linguistic behaviour. For example, in many Western cultures, people wear black at funerals, whereas in some Eastern cultures, people are more likely to wear white. These associations often become encoded in language and are then perpetuated through linguistic behaviour. For this reason, it is difficult to disentangle linguistic and cultural influences. It is generally acknowledged that emotion–colour associations originate from several overlapping and interlinked sources, including bodily based experiences, environmental features, and linguistic and cultural factors. For instance, in their large-scale investigation of emotion–colour associations based on a sample of thirty nations speaking twenty-two native languages, Jonauskaite and colleagues (2020) showed that the majority of associations that were reported could be seen in all the languages that they investigated (average similarity coefficient r = .88). However, they also found some local differences, and conclude from these differences that widespread tendencies to associate certain colours with certain emotions may be further modulated by cultural and individual factors. They argue that a colour like red, for instance, may be associated with both negative or positive emotions, depending on whether the speaker comes from a Western country or from China (Jonauskaite et al. 2019b). They suggest that the existence of both types of association can be explained in evolutionary terms, for example, by the fact that red is associated with blood, and thus connotes both danger and sexuality. They suggest that some of these evolutionary-based associations are further developed in certain cultures. Jonauskaite and colleagues assume for example that the Chinese cultural belief that red is a symbol of good fortune has probably strengthened the evolutionary link between the colour red and positive emotions (see also Wang, Shu & Mo, 2014). In contrast, the particularly strong association that is found between the colour red and danger in countries such as the United States (Pravossoudovitch et al., 2014) may strengthen the links between red and negative feelings, while weakening the links between red and positive feelings such as love and passion.

The fact that variation has been found in the types of association that people form is not surprising, given that the ways in which people talk about (and possibly perceive) both emotions and colours are susceptible to both cross-linguistic and cross-cultural variation. The fact that people's perceptions of both emotions and colours vary across cultures makes it highly likely that there will also be variation in the associations that people form between the two. In the next two sections, we explore each of these types of variation in turn. We refer to 'cross-linguistic' and 'cross-cultural' throughout these sections for the sake of brevity, while remaining cognisant of the fact that the two are inextricably linked.

1.4.1 Cross-Linguistic and Cross-Cultural Variation in the Ways in Which People Perceive and Describe Emotion

In the opening sections of this introduction, we saw that cultural and linguistic environments play an important role in shaping the ways in which people understand and communicate emotions. One would therefore expect a degree of variation between cultures in the ways in which emotions are expressed and in the colours that are associated with them. Considerable differences have indeed been observed in the ways in which people from different cultures talk about emotions. Heelas (1996) shows that people from different cultures vary in terms of the number of emotions that they can clearly identify, what those emotions mean, how they are classified and evaluated, where in the body they are thought to be 'located', the kinds of occurrences that are thought to generate particular emotions, the powers that are ascribed to particular emotions, and the ways in which emotions are managed (p. 171). Like Barrett (2017a,b), Heelas argues that emotional experiences are largely shaped by the social and cultural contexts in which they occur. He introduces the idea of 'hyper-cognised' emotions, which tend to be given high cultural value, and contribute to the distinctiveness of particular cultures. An example of a culturally specific emotional construct is the Javanese term 'liget', which according to Rosaldo (1980), has the following qualities:

> *Liget* is associated most readily with a variety of words suggesting chaos, separation, and confusion, words that point to the disruptive qualities of anger uncontrolled by 'knowledge' – 'anger' that derives from someone else's fury or success. Red ornaments, signifying the *liget* of a killer . . . and red in the Sky at sunset is a form of *liget* that can make people feel ill. (Rosaldo, 1980, p. 47)

It is interesting to observe the references to colour in this citation. The fact that 'liget' is associated with the colour red suggests that it is something akin to what might be termed 'anger' in English. However, Rosaldo goes on to point out that when 'liget' is given some form of focus, it can take on much more positive characteristics:

> Concentrated *liget* is what makes babies, stirs one on to work . . . gives people strength and courage, narrows vision on a victim or a task. (Rosaldo, 1980, p. 49)

Here the term 'liget' appears to have elements of what we might describe in English as 'drive' or 'passion'. In terms of emotion–colour correspondences, one might expect culturally important emotions to be associated more strongly with colours than less important emotions.

Another source of potential variation is the way in which emotions are somatised; in other words, the way in which they are talked about in relation to parts of the body. This may be in terms of organs that cannot literally be felt (such as the liver) or as parts of the body that can be felt (such as the stomach or the eye). The location of the emotions in different parts of the body may also affect the colours that they are associated with, with more centrally located emotions being more likely to be represented by the colour red than emotions that are located in, for example, the eyes.

The idea that the way in which emotions are talked about affects the way in which they are experienced relates to the theory of linguistic relativity, which we discuss below in Section 1.4.2. Regardless of whether the variation remains at the level of language or whether it penetrates the experience of emotion, it is likely to have an impact on the ways in which people from different cultures associate emotions with colours. Variation in the number of emotions that are perceived may impact on the way in which the colour spectrum is divided up to correspond to different emotions. In addition to the emotions themselves, the ways in which the emotions are evaluated is also likely to affect the colours with which they are associated. We saw earlier that more positive emotions are more likely to be associated with lighter colours, but the extent to which emotions are perceived as 'positive' may vary from culture to culture. In addition, the kinds of experiences that are thought to provoke particular emotions may also have an effect, as the environments in which those experiences occurred may have metonymic links to certain colours.

To sum up, there are numerous ways in which the description, and possibly by extension the experience of emotion varies across languages and cultures. These all have the potential to shape the associations that people from different linguistic and cultural backgrounds form between emotions and colours. The picture becomes even more complex when we consider the ways in which colour description and perception varies across cultures. It is to this subject that we now turn.

1.4.2 Cross-Linguistic and Cross-Cultural Variation in the Ways in Which People Perceive and Describe Colour

There is a substantial amount of work showing that cultures vary in terms of how they divide up the colour spectrum. Work in this area dates back to 1969 when Berlin and Kay (1969) found that different languages employ very different sets of colour terms. They found that more technologically advanced cultures developed more colour terms. Berlin and Kay argue that despite the apparent diversity across languages and cultures, colour terms tend to emerge following a natural order. They argue that this order emanates from an innately specified sequence of basic colour terms and that the inventory of colour terms in each

white   red   green   blue   brown   **purple**
black   yellow   pink
                                                 orange
                                                 grey

Figure 1 The 'hierarchy' of colour terms proposed by Berlin and Kay (1969)

language is not random or arbitrary. The hierarchy is shown in Figure 1, which runs from left to right, with black and white being the most basic colour terms followed by red, then green and yellow, then blue, then brown and finally purple, pink, orange and grey.

Berlin and Kay found that most languages have terms for these eleven basic colours, but some languages were found to have only a subset of these terms. For example, the language Dani, which is spoken in New Guinea, was found to only have two colour terms: 'mili' (black) and 'mola' (white). This led to the question of whether people whose language only has a restricted number of colour terms are able to conceptualise colours beyond these two terms. Berlin and Kay found that despite not having words for other colours, speakers of Dani in New Guinea were in fact able to categorise other colours besides black and white. In terms of emotion–colour associations, one might think that associations that involve basic colour terms may be more widely shared than associations involving other colours. However, it is important to note that in recent years, the idea that there are basic colour terms has received a substantial amount of criticism, first because it is based on English, which biases the findings with respect to other languages, and second because Berlin and Kay relied heavily on second-hand sources and had no first-hand knowledge of many of the languages that they studied.

More recent work on cross-linguistic and cross-cultural variation in colour terms has focused on subtle differences between shades of colour that are named in some languages but not in others. The most widely researched distinction in this area involves the so-called 'Russian blue'. Speakers of Russian have two different words for two different shades of blue: 'goluboy' (light blue) and 'siniy' (dark blue).[2] Winawer and colleagues (2007) investigated whether this distinction makes speakers of Russian more able to distinguish between these two shades of blue than speakers of English. In their

---

[2] This distinction exists in other languages too, such as Italian, Greek and Korean, but the research investigating the impact that the linguistic distinction has on perceptual categorization has been conducted only on Russian speakers. In Italian, for instance, there are three basic terms that refer to 3 different shades of blue: 'blu' (dark blue), 'azzurro' (medium blue, as the colour of the national Italian football team, 'gli Azzurri') and 'celeste' (a light shade of blue, comparable to baby blue).

study, they invited speakers of English and Russian to look at a 'siniy'-coloured square. They then showed pairs of other squares in different shades of blue and asked them to indicate which shade was equal to that of the prompt square. In some cases, the distractor square was 'goluboy' and in others it was another shade of blue. Winawer and colleagues found a relative advantage in the Russian speakers for the prompt involving the shade of blue that corresponds to 'goluboy', in comparison with the other shades of blue. The speakers of English showed no such advantage, which suggests that the fact that Russian speakers have names for these two shades of blue makes them more likely to attend to the distinction than speakers of languages that do not have this distinction. This finding (and others like it) provides support for the idea that the language that people speak can help to direct their interactions with the physical world, as they are more likely to notice (or at least see the relevance of) features and category boundaries that are encoded in their own particular language than ones that are not (Macnamara, 2019). This idea is related to the so-called 'linguistic relativity' hypothesis that the language we speak shapes the way we think (Sapir, 1929; Whorf, 1940). Although the strong version of this hypothesis has been widely refuted, there is now an extensive body of empirical work whose findings show that the language we speak can direct our attention towards some features in the natural environment and make us less likely to notice others (Niemeier & Dirven, 2000; Pütz & Verspoor, 2000; Slobin, 1996). The focus of more nuanced recent work in the area is on identifying and understanding the factors that contribute to the extent of and the nature of influences that language has been observed to have on perception (Athanasopoulos & Casaponsa, 2020).

These findings suggest that variation in emotion–colour associations may be explained by both linguistic differences and broader cultural differences. As we saw earlier, the two dimensions are strongly linked and both are likely to play a role; sometimes language will be the driving force of the variation, and sometimes culture.

To sum up, the colour spectrum appears to be divided up in subtly different ways across different cultures and this affects the way in which people perceive colours particularly when they are thinking about them using language. The fact that there are linguistic and cultural differences in the ways in which colours themselves are perceived may have an impact on the ways in which they are associated with different emotions. The conclusion from this section and Section 1.3 is that variation in perceptual, linguistic, cultural and environmental experiences of both emotion and colour are likely to combine to shape the associations that people form between emotions and colours.

1.5 Variation in Emotion–Colour Associations Depending on the Gender in Which the Emotional Descriptor is Presented

So far we have discussed the ways in which emotions and colours, and the associations that are formed between them, vary across languages and cultures. There is however another potentially important source of variation: the gender in which the emotional descriptor (i.e. the prompt) is presented. Differences have been observed in the ways in which men and women are 'expected' to experience both emotions and colours. These differences are, to a large extent, socially constructed and reflect societal expectations of gendered behaviour. According to social role theory, beliefs about gender are based on perceptions of the communal and agentic attributes of men and women (Eagly & Wood, 1991). Communal attributes, such as affection, sensitivity and sympathy are more strongly ascribed to women, while agentic attributes, such as dominance, ambition and aggression are more strongly ascribed to men. Women are expected to display emotions such as happiness, calmness and shyness, while men are expected to exhibit 'stronger' emotions, such as anger, fury and confidence. In many societies, women have a much narrower behavioural range within which it is socially acceptable for them to operate, especially when it comes to strong negative emotions, such as anger (Eagly & Wood, 1991). It is deemed more acceptable for men to display strong negative emotions than it is for women to do so.

Differences in the ways in which the emotional lives of men and women are perceived may affect the colour choices that people make when the emotional adjectives are used to describe men and women respectively. In some languages, the adjectival description of the emotion alters according to whether it is referring to a man or a woman. For example, in Italian, the word for 'joyful' is 'allegro' or 'allegra', depending on whether it refers to a man or a woman. One might predict that more saturated colours will be selected for negative emotions when they are presented in the masculine grammatical form than when they are represented in the feminine grammatical form. Conversely, if it is the case that women are meant to be more joyful than men, then participants may associate the emotion with a lighter shade of yellow when it is applied to a woman ('allegra') than when it is used to refer to a man ('allegro'). In other words, when an emotional descriptor is presented in the feminine form, participants may form a set of associations that is different from those that they will form when it is presented in the masculine form, and this may affect the colours that people associate with emotion words when they appear in different grammatical genders. They may select lighter and more muted colours when the adjective appears in the feminine form.

Indirect support for this hypothesis comes from the finding that grammatical gender affects people's perception of concrete objects. Findings from research employing a range of different paradigms (voice attribution, trait attribution and inference generation tasks) have shown that grammatical gender affects the content of conceptual representations of objects that do not have an actual gender (Sato & Athanasopoulos, 2018). In Spanish, the word for 'bridge', *el puente*, is masculine, whereas the word in German, *die Brücke*, is feminine. Boroditsky and Schmidt (2000) found that Spanish and German speakers' memory for object–name pairs (e.g. 'bridge-Antonio') was better for pairs where the gender of the proper name was congruent with the grammatical gender of the object name (in their native language), than when the two genders were incongruent. This was true even though both groups performed the task in English. These findings suggest that grammatical gender can shape thinking. Indeed, grammatical gender has been frequently employed to fuel the long-lasting debate on linguistic relativity (for a review, see Cubelli, Paolieri, Lotto & Job, 2011).

To sum up, findings from the research literature suggest that, to some extent, men and women are perceived to have different internal emotional lives. These differences may lead to differences in the colours that people associate with adjectives relating to emotions, depending on whether they are presented in the masculine or the feminine form.

1.6 Our Study and Its Research Questions

In the preceding discussion, several research questions have emerged, along with their corresponding hypotheses. These questions relate to the nature of the emotion–colour associations that people form in relation to the saturation, lightness and hue of colours, the reasons that they provide for them, and variation in the kinds of associations that people make. In this Element we present the findings from a study in which we explore the relationship between emotions and colours in depth.

The research questions are as follows:

RQ1. What are the strongest emotion–colour associations overall, and how do emotion–colour associations vary according to linguistic background?

Here we aim to identify the strongest emotion–colour associations and look at how these associations vary according to the linguistic backgrounds of the participants. We aim to establish whether there are any associations that are particularly likely to be favoured by participants with a specific linguistic/cultural background. We included participants from six linguistic backgrounds:

British English, American English, Spanish, German, Italian and Cantonese. We had several reasons for selecting these languages and cultures. Firstly, the selection allowed us to compare languages from several different language families (Romance, Germanic and Sino Tibetan), to include languages and cultures that exhibit linguistic and geographical proximity and remoteness, and to compare two varieties of the same language (British and American English). The inclusion of Spanish and Italian also allowed us to compare participants' responses to emotional adjectives that were presented in the masculine or feminine gender. German also has grammatical gender. With respect to adjectives there is, however, a neutral uninflected form (e.g. 'grün', 'green') that is used for adjectives in isolation as opposed to when the adjective is used in attributive form. In the study, we have used this neutral, uninflected form. At least one member of the research team was a native speaker of each of these languages.

RQ2. How do emotional valence and intensity map onto colour lightness and saturation, and how do these relationships vary according to linguistic background of the participant and the grammatical gender of the emotion?[3]

Here we use normed data for each of the emotion terms to investigate whether there are any relationships between the intensity and valence of an emotion and the saturation and lightness of the colours that people associate with it. Our hypothesis is that colours with higher intensity ratings will be associated with more saturated colours and that colours with high valence ratings will be associated with lighter colours. We investigate whether and if so, how these associations vary according to the linguistic background of the participant, and postulate reasons for the kinds of variation that we find. We also explore whether responses vary according to the gender of the prompt, hypothesising that emotions presented in the female gender will be associated with brighter and less saturated colours. To investigate this phenomenon, we manipulate the gender used in the prompt in languages that require this (for example, 'angry' in Spanish, is *enfadada* when applied to a woman and *enfadado* when applied to a man).

RQ3. What reasons do people provide for emotion–colour associations and how do these reasons vary according to the linguistic background, the emotion being discussed, and the colour being selected? If an association is bodily related, is it more likely to be widely shared?

---

[3] We also investigated the effect that the gender of the participants had on the emotion–colour associations that they formed. We do not have space to report the findings from that part of the study in this Element, but they can be found in the supplementary materials, along with a short theoretical justification for that part of the study.

Here we explore the reasons that participants provide when explaining emotion–colour associations. We also investigate the extent to which and the ways in which these reasons vary according to the linguistic backgrounds of the participants, the emotion being discussed, and the colour being selected. We begin by identifying the most common motivations and investigate whether there are any motivations that are particularly strongly related to a specific linguistic background. We also investigate whether participants from similar linguistic backgrounds (e.g. Spanish and Italian) behave similarly, in terms of the type of explanations they provide for emotion–colour associations. We then go on to investigate how the emotions and colours vary in terms of the explanations that they 'attract'. We use the findings from this part of the study to identify over-arching characteristics of emotions and colours that tend to attract similar kinds of explanations. We then compare the frequency of a particular association with its primary explanation type, in order to answer the question: If an association is bodily related, is it more widely attested?

2 Methodology

2.1 Introduction

In our study, participants were presented with a series of emotional terms and asked to select the colour that they believed was associated most closely to each of the terms, and to provide reasons for their choices. In this section, we provide demographic information about our participants. We then explain the rationale for the emotions and colours used in the study. We explain how the emotions were coded for valence and intensity and how the colours were coded for lightness and saturation. We then provide details of the questionnaire itself. Finally, we provide a detailed account of the ways in which we annotated the participants' free text responses in which they explained their motivations for the different emotion–colour associations that they had made.

2.2 Participants

In total, 568 participants took part in the study. Table 1 shows the number of participants with respect to language/culture and gender. All participants were eighteen years of age or above. The age range was from eighteen to seventy-four and the mean age was thirty-two.

In our study, we invited speakers of five different languages to tell us about the colours that they associated with particular emotions. The five languages investigated were English, Spanish, Italian, German and Cantonese. We included two varieties of English: British English and North American English. Participants were residents in Britain, The United States of America, Spain, Italy, Germany and Hong

Table 1 Distribution of participants (N = 568) according to language and gender

	American English	British English	Cantonese	German	Italian	Spanish
Female	54	31	53	41	79	61
Male	30	29	33	34	63	60

Kong. Discussions of the factors that shape emotion–colour associations often make reference to lingiustic and cultural factors, and indeed, as we will see later in the Element, we found evidence of both in our study. It can be difficult to disentangle the impact of language and culture, which means that differences that we found between our groups of participants might be explained by the language (or variety of language) that they speak or the culture with which that language is associated. When labelling the different groups of participants, it was therefore difficult to find a term that would cover all these possibilities yet remain concise enough to allow for repeated use throughout the Element. We have chosen to use the term 'linguistic background' for the sake of simplicity, but we understand this to encompass both the languages and varieties of languages under investigation (as in the case of British and North American English) and the cultural characteristics that are associated with those languages. We therefore refer to our groups as having six 'linguistic backgrounds': British English, American English, Spanish, Italian, German and Cantonese. At times, for the sake of brevity we refer to 'British English', 'American English', 'Spanish', 'Italian', 'German' and 'Cantonese' participants.

In order for the study to have sufficient power for our planned statistical analyses, we aimed to have at least thirty participants in the first four language groups (American English, British English, Cantonese and German) and twice this number of participants for Spanish and Italian, as in these languages we had two versions of the questionnaire (one with the emotions presented in the masculine form and one with the emotions presented in the feminine form).[4] However, because the questionnaire was distributed largely via social media, we managed to recruit more than the minimum number of participants in many of the categories.

2.3 Questionnaire Design

The data were collected through an online questionnaire designed in Qualtrics and distributed through Facebook, Twitter and Prolific. Participants (N = 568) were shown fifteen words for emotions (angry, bored, calm, cheerful, confident,

---

[4] During data analysis, one participant from the British English group had to be discarded because his/her age was below 18. This is why we only have 29 participants rather than 30 in this group.

depressed, excited, fearful, furious, happy, jealous, joyful, passionate, sad and shy) one after the other, in their own language. For each emotion, they were asked to choose from a set of twenty-five colours the colour they most strongly associated with that emotion. Details of the questionnaire are provided in Section 2.3.3.

2.3.1 Selection of Emotions for Inclusion in the Study

The emotions that we included in the study were: angry, bored, calm, cheerful, confident, depressed, excited, fearful, furious, happy, jealous, joyful, passionate, sad and shy. These emotions were elicited from speakers in a focus group (N = 10) during which they were asked to think of positive and negative emotions that they would possibly associate with colours. Confirmation that these emotions have indeed been found to be associated with colours was sought through a review of the literature on emotion–colour associations (Aslam, 2006; Barchard, Grob & Roe, 2017; Chen, Kacinik, Chen & Wu, 2016; Clarke & Costall, 2008; Deabler, 1957; Fraser & Banks, 2004; Fugate & Franco, 2019; Gorn, Chattopadhyay, Yi & Dahl, 1997; Jonauskaite et al., 2020; Soriano & Valenzuela, 2009; Walters, Apter & Svebak, 1982; Wexner, 1954). As a consequence, the emotions that we analysed do not necessarily reflect the emotions listed in any particular theoretical model (e.g. Ekman, 1992).

In order to test whether emotional adjectives are associated with different colours when presented in the masculine or feminine form, we included two languages in the study that mark their adjectives as either masculine or feminine (i.e. Italian and Spanish). For these languages, two versions of the questionnaire were distributed, one containing masculine adjectives and one containing feminine adjectives. For example, for the emotion 'angry', there were two versions of the questionnaire in Italian, containing 'arrabbiato' and 'arrabbiata', and two in Spanish, containing 'enfadado' and 'enfadada'. A list of the emotion terms included in the study is shown in Table 2.

The emotion terms were first selected in English since this was the working language of the team. Translations of the English terms into Cantonese, German, Italian and Spanish were based on dictionary definitions. Furthermore, for each language three native speakers who were also highly proficient in English were consulted in order to provide their preferred translation for the respective term. Among these translations we selected the one most frequently provided for each term.

We identified the valence and intensity ratings for each of these emotions using Warriner, Kuperman and Brysbaert's (2013) semantic-affective

Table 2 The fifteen emotion terms used in the questionnaire

	Emotion (English)	Emotion (Cantonese)	Emotion (German)	Emotion (Italian)	Emotion (Spanish)
1	Angry	生氣 [sang1] [hei3]	Verärgert	Arrabbiato/a	Enfadado/a
2	Bored	沉悶 [cham4] [mun6]	Gelangweilt	Annoiata/o	Aburrida/o
3	Calm	冷靜 [laang5] [jing6]	Ruhig	Calma/o	Tranquila/o
4	Cheerful	愉快 [yu4] [faai3]	Fröhlich	Allegra/o	Alegre
5	Confident	自信 [ji6] [seun3]	Selbstbewusst	Sicura/o	Segura/o (de sí misma/o)
6	Depressed	抑鬱 [yik1] [wat1]	Deprimiert	Depressa/o	Deprimida/o
7	Excited	興奮 [hing1] [fan5]	Aufgeregt (in Vorfreude)	Entusiasta/o	Entusiasmada/o
8	Fearful	憂慮 [yau1] [leui6]	Ängstlich	Timorosa/o	Miedosa/o
9	Furious	憤怒 [fan5] [nou6]	Wütend	Furiosa/o	Furiosa/o
10	Happy	快樂 [faai3] [lok6]	Glücklich	Felice	Feliz

Table 2 (cont.)

	Emotion (English)	Emotion (Cantonese)	Emotion (German)	Emotion (Italian)	Emotion (Spanish)
11	Jealous	妒忌 [dou3] [gei6]	Neidisch (a) Eifersüchtig (b)[5]	Gelosa/o	Celosa/o
12	Joyful	高興 [goul] [hing3]	Freudig	Gioiosa/o	Risueña/o
13	Passionate	熱情 [yit6] [ching4]	Leidenschaftlich	Appassionata/o	Apasionada/o
14	Sad	傷心 [seung1] [sam1]	Traurig	Triste	Triste
15	Shy	害羞 [hoi6] [sau1]	Schüchtern	Timida/o	Tímida/o

[5] The meaning of English 'jealous' encompasses meanings that can be expressed by two different terms in German: 'eifersüchtig', which primarily refers to the emotion of being upset because you think someone who you love is attracted to someone else; and 'neidisch', which refers to being unhappy because someone has, or can do, something that you would like to have or do (both meaning descriptions are taken from the entry for 'jealous' in the Macmillan Dictionary). The latter meaning overlaps with English 'envious'. Although this lexico-semantic overlap also exists in Spanish and Italian; when we asked informants to provide translations for the English emotion terms, only the German informants provided different translations for 'jealous'. For this reason, we decided to include both terms, 'eifersüchtig' and 'neidisch', in the questionnaire for our German participants. Differences in responses between the two terms are discussed in Section 3.

norms. They asked native speakers to rate 13,000 English words on a nine-point scale for valence (which they define as the inherent degree of positivity or negativity of the word) and arousal (which they define as the 'intensity' of the emotion provoked by a word).[6] For valence, participants were asked to rate the words on a scale from 'unhappy' to 'happy' and for arousal, they were asked to rate the words on a scale from 'calm' to 'excited'. We therefore use their measure of 'arousal' as a proxy for the perceived 'intensity' of the emotion, although we are aware of the fact that the two terms are not identical (see Reisenzein, 1994), as, strictly speaking, arousal refers to the strength of the response in the automatic nervous system. Because of the specific physiological meaning that is conveyed by the word 'arousal', we employ the term 'intensity' throughout our study. Table 3 shows the mean values for valence and intensity for the fifteen

Table 3 Mean valence and intensity ratings for the emotion terms used in the questionnaire (9 is 'high', 1 is 'low')

Emotion	Valence	Intensity
Angry	2.53	6.20
Bored	2.95	3.65
Calm	6.89	1.67
Cheerful	8.00	5.76
Confident	7.56	4.62
Depressed	2.27	4.25
Excited	8.11	6.43
Fearful	2.66	5.45
Furious	2.57	6.09
Happy	8.47	6.05
Jealous	2.38	5.90
Joyful	8.21	5.53
Passionate	7.17	6.33
Sad	2.10	3.49
Shy	5.16	3.33

---

[6] The terms 'arousal' and 'intensity' are sometimes used interchangeably. Montefinese, Ambrosini, Fairfield, & Mammarella (2014, p. 888) state that 'arousal, also termed 'intensity' or 'energy level', expresses the degree of excitement or activation an individual feels toward a given stimulus, varies from calm to exciting'. We hereby adopt their definition of arousal, conscious that in the field of neurophsysiology it is defined slightly differently, with arousal referring explicitly to the magnitude of a person's physiological response to a stimulus or event.

emotions selected for this study, for English. Ratings of emotional valence and intensity have also been collected for other languages, including the languages analysed in the present study: Italian (Montefinese et al., 2014), Cantonese (Yee, 2017), German (Schmidtke et al., 2014) and Spanish (Redondo et al., 2007). However, in order to facilitate comparison of the results across languages, we used a single set of measures in our analysis. We chose to use the English measures because the original set of stimuli used in the study were in English and then we translated such stimuli in other languages, using native speakers' intuitions, as described before. Moreover, studies in which ratings are provided for Italian, German, Spanish and Cantonese show high correlations with the valence and intensity ratings collected for English.

2.3.2 Selection of Colours for Inclusion in the Study

Twenty-five colours were selected for inclusion in the study, covering the entire colour spectrum. We believed that twenty-five items would provide sufficient nuance to the study and allow us to investigate the roles played by saturation and lightness, but without overwhelming participants by giving them too many colours to choose from. The saturation and lightness values for each of these colours are shown in Table 4.

Since in Italian and Spanish the names for the emotions are grammatically inflected for grammatical gender (either masculine or feminine), we devised two different questionnaires: one with the emotion terms in their masculine form, and one for the emotion terms in their feminine form. We thus obtained roughly twice as much data from Italian and Spanish participants: at least thirty participants of each gender for each questionnaire (see Table 5).

2.3.3 The Questionnaire

For each emotion, participants were asked to choose from a set of twenty-five colours the colour they most strongly associated with that emotion. Participants could only select one colour, which they did so by clicking on the corresponding coloured pencil (Figure 2). This was a compulsory part of the task and they were not able to move to the next screen unless they had chosen one colour (or one of the two text options: 'colour not listed here' or 'no association').

Table 4 Saturation and lightness values for the colours used in the questionnaire

Colour	Saturation (%)	Lightness (%)
White	0	100
Sun yellow	80	92
Gold yellow	80	91
Orange	85	89
Ruby red	93	85
Blood red	76	78
Pomegranate red	89	53
Wine red	34	39
Pink	35	90
Lavender purple	29	75
Violet purple	36	52
Baby blue	49	93
Sky blue	72	77
Sea Blue	85	58
Ink blue	67	34
Turquoise	35	62
Apple green	77	75
Grass green	66	50

Table 4 (cont.)

		34	31
	Bottle green	34	31
	Toffee brown	50	88
	Cinnamon brown	76	63
	Sand brown	56	46
	Chocolate brown	35	22
	Grey	2	56
	Black	7	11

Table 5 Distribution of Italian and Spanish participants with respect to gender and type of questionnaire.

	Italian		Spanish	
	Feminine forms	Masculine forms	Feminine forms	Masculine forms
Female participants	38	41	30	31
Male participants	30	33	30	30

Colour not listed here
No association

Figure 2 The prompt that was presented to the participants.

The exact wording was as follows:

> **Welcome!**
>
> *In this survey, you will be shown a series of words for feelings. For each feeling:*[7]
>
> - *If you think it is associated with a colour, click on the corresponding coloured pencil below. You can only choose one colour per set of pencils. When you have chosen a colour, please type your reason for that choice in the text box below. If you identify a colour but cannot think of any specific reason, or if you cannot find any colour that applies, please write 'no explanation' in the box below.*
> - *If you do not think there is a colour association, click on one of the corresponding text options below: Colour not listed here (if you think that the feeling is associated with a colour but you cannot find it among the pencils) or No association (if you cannot think of a colour association for that feeling).*

As well as being asked to select a colour for an emotion term, participants were given the option to select 'colour not listed here' or 'no association'. Participants were thus able to select from a range of **twenty-seven** potential answers (twenty-five colours plus 'colour not listed here' or 'no association'). If they selected 'colour not listed' they were not asked to name or describe an alternative colour as it would have been difficult to identify an exact shade from their description.

Participants were then invited to explain their choice of colour for each emotion in the form of a free text response. Below the picture of the pencils, participants saw a textbox with a heading that combined the emotion term in the heading and the statement 'reasons for your choice'. This option was not compulsory, and participants could move to the next screen without writing their responses.

There was no time limit to the questionnaire. Participants did not receive any monetary compensation for participation. They were informed that the data would be stored securely in a password-protected electronic system for three years after the end of the study in line with European data protection rules. They were also informed that the data would be destroyed after that date. The project was approved by the Ethics Committee at the University of Birmingham, UK (ERN_16-0608AP14).

---

[7] We chose to use the word 'feeling' in our questionnaire rather than 'emotion' as our informal piloting showed that its meaning was more accessible for participants.

Angry. Reason for your choice:

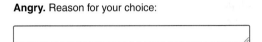

Figure 3 Prompt asking participants to provide reason for their choice of colour

2.4 Identifying Motivation Types

As stated in Section 2.3.3, for each emotion, participants were asked to provide a reason for their choice of associated colour, in the form of a free text response. For each item in the questionnaire, below the picture of the pencils, participants saw the prompt that is shown in Figure 3. They wrote their response in their own language. This option was not compulsory and participants could move to the next screen without writing a reason.

The reasons offered for their choices were coded into five broad categories: bodily based motivation, cross-modal correspondence, environmentally based motivation, linguistic (idiomatic) motivation, and unclear/unsure. The category 'environmentally based motivation' was further subdivided into 'natural physical environment' and 'man-made or culturally mediated physical environment' and the category 'linguistic (idiomatic) motivation' was further subdivided into the categories 'bodily based idiom' and 'non-bodily based idiom'. Motivation types were only coded when they were explicitly stated in the response.

Responses were coded as **'bodily based'** if they made a clear reference to bodily function or feature. Answers in this category were often metonymic in that they invoked a direct cause–effect relationship (e.g. 'Red face when angry') but sometimes they shaded into metaphor (e.g. 'Because there is fire inside you'; 'Because you shine when you are happy'). Answers that drew on folk anatomy were also included in this category (e.g. 'I think of jealousy as more associated with yellow bile').

Responses were coded as involving a **'cross-modal correspondence'** if they involved some sort of mapping between the emotion and the colour, which made reference to the intensity, valence, or the complexity of the emotion and to the visual properties of the colours (e.g. 'deep red speaks to me of intensity, which I associate with passionate'; 'I think brighter colours represent cheerful more. And the light yellow is the most bright'). Often the colours appeared to be 'personified' in some way (e.g. 'That blue is blue and proud!'; 'yellow is bright, outgoing'; 'dark red seems like a very unapologetic colour', 'a vindictive colour'; 'Furiousness has a single-mindedness to it that can only be black'; 'The colour feels enthusiastic, like it will lift you up'). The answers in this category differed from those in the 'bodily based' category as participants did not simply invoke a metonymic cause–effect relationship (e.g. 'I go blue when

I'm cold'). Instead, participants appeared to be operating on a more metaphorical level, identifying two different entities and seeking similarities between them. For example, responses in this category often involved comparisons with similar emotions and colours, as participants sought to explain why they had chosen a particular shade of a colour for a particular emotion (e.g. 'Fury is darker than anger – anger burns bright and more on the surface than fury'; 'harsh colour, brighter than for angry – shows higher level of anger').

Responses were coded as '**referring to the natural physical environment**' if they made reference to the natural physical environment but not to the human body. They usually made reference to human responses to environmental features (e.g. 'I associate grey, rainy weather and rain is like sadness'; 'bright and exciting, the colour of heat'; 'bright colour and association with the sun and it being a mood raiser').

Responses were coded as '**referring to the man-made or culturally mediated environment**' if they made reference to man-made artefacts, such as traffic signs, or references to culture (e.g. 'I think of a bull seeing red and red mist causing anger'; 'I associate dark red with the word passion because of the colour of red roses & the link with the word "passion" & "romantic love:"'; '[Black is] quite an established colour, used often with high-status such as police officers/navy etc.'; '[Pink] It's feminine'; 'White flag for peace'; 'Suicide and revenge need to wear red', in reference to the traditional association between red and jealousy in Hong Kong).

Responses were coded as '**involving bodily based linguistic (idiomatic) expressions**' if they referred to an idiom that had a clear and motivated connection to a bodily function. For example, the participant response 'seeing red is what I see when I'm angry' refers to the idiom 'seeing red', but it also relates to the fact that people become red when they are angry.

Responses were coded as '**involving non-bodily based linguistic (idiomatic) expressions**' if they referred to an idiom that did not have a clear and motivated connection to a bodily function. These responses could not be traced back to any bodily related origin and were deemed to have stemmed solely from language or culture. For example, the participant response 'The blues for sad' refers to the culturally based description of a style of music but it does not relate in a clear and motivated way to a bodily function – people do not literally turn blue when they are sad. Similarly, the participant who replied, 'The expression "green with envy" – Shakespeare?' is referring to an idiom that he/she thinks may have originated in Shakespeare's writing but there is no clear connection to a bodily function: people do not literally turn green when they are envious or jealous.

Responses were coded as '**unclear**' when the motivation was not explicitly stated or when there was insufficient information to allow the coder to say for sure what the motivation was. Sometimes participants simply reported that associations were conventional (e.g. 'I've always heard that jealousy is yellow'). At other times, they simply stated that they liked a particular colour (e.g. 'My favourite colour') or said that they associated the emotion with a particular colour without saying why (e.g. 'I associate pink with emotion cheery').

Responses were coded as '**don't know**' when participants wrote things like 'no explanation', 'don't know', 'not sure' or 'no reason'. When participants provided no answer at all, this was also coded as belonging to this category.

Some of the responses were difficult to categorise as they were on the cusp of two or more different categories. For example, the answer 'Anger feels like an erupting volcano, so the red lava colour is what I think of', could be coded as bodily based or as relating to the natural physical environment. We coded this particular example as relating to the natural physical environment as the idea of the volcano contributed most of the meaning here. Other responses made references to human interactions with the environment (e.g. 'Brown – if you feel shy you may want to blend in or camouflage yourself'; 'Black because people are scared of darkness'). Although we could have coded such responses as 'bodily based', we decided to code them as environmentally based in order to distinguish them from the purely bodily based responses and because all the responses that referred to the environment made reference, on some level, to the affordances that it offers humans. As we will see in our analysis of these motivations in Section 5, all the response types (from 1–4) involved a complex interplay between metaphorical and metonymic reasoning, with the respective roles played by these two types of reasoning, and the nature of the interaction between them, fluctuating across the different examples.

Table 6 Categories of response types with examples

Type of response	Example
1. Bodily based motivation	'Because when you are angry you sometimes feel the blood rush to your head/face' (Angry is red)
2. Cross-modal correspondence	'The blue is blue and proud' (Passionate is blue)
3. Environmentally based motivation	
3a. Natural physical environment	'Reminds me of sunshine' (Joyful is yellow)
3b. Man-made or culturally mediated physical environment	'Ice cream brands always use pink and donut places' (Excited is pink)

Table 6 (cont.)

Type of response	Example
4. Linguistic (idiomatic) motivation	
4a. Bodily based idiom	'Seeing red is what I say when I'm angry' (Angry is red)
4b. Non-bodily based idiom	'The metaphor feeling blue is often used to describe someone who is sad' (Sad is blue)
5. No clear motivation provided	
5a. Unclear motivation	'My favourite colour' (Yellow is joyful)
5b. Don't know	'No reason' (Joyful is yellow)

A full list of the categories, with examples, is shown in Table 6.

The coding of responses was undertaken in three stages. In the first stage, all five researchers annotated the same sample of texts (these were taken from the English data) in order to establish the coding scheme. The second stage consisted of two rounds of annotation designed to measure and improve the reliability of the scheme. In the first round, six coders (the five authors of the Element plus an external coder) annotated 100 responses from the English dataset (as this was the working language of the team). Overall, we reached a moderate agreement between the annotations of the researchers, although the inter-rater reliability for the main categories (bodily based, cross-modal, environmental, idiomatic and unclear) was slightly higher (Krippendorf's alpha: 0.671) than for the full coding scheme involving sub-categories (Krippendorf's alpha: 0.589) (Krippendorff, 2011).[8] After the first round, all the researchers met for a joint discussion of cases where there was disagreement to clarify the protocol and introduce refinements where needed. The second round of annotation only involved the five researchers in the team and an additional set of 100 open answers from the English dataset. Both inter-rater reliability scores increased (only main categories: 0.733; including sub-categories: 0.655), showing that the joint discussion of annotations between rounds had resulted in the coherent use of the protocol by the team of researchers. In the third phase, each researcher annotated the full dataset of responses in their corresponding mother tongue using the protocol that we have just described.

---

[8] Krippendorf's alpha is a general statistic measure of inter-rater reliability for coding protocols involving more than two coders and for cases where there are more than two possible options to annotate each item.

Once the data had been collected, a range of statistical analyses were conducted in order to answer the research questions outlined in Section 1. All the tests were performed in the R environment (R version 3.6.3, 2020–02-29). We used the 'dplyr' package for data treatment, 'lme4' for the mixed linear regression models, 'lsa' for calculating the distances between languages, based on the colour-feeling associations provided by the participants, and 'ggplot2' to plot the graphs. The full dataset (including the researchers' annotations for the motivations) and the statistical scripts are available in a public online repository: https://osf.io/xb8yt/.

In Sections 3 to 6, we present the findings to our research questions. In each case, we outline the statistical tests that were performed and provide a rationale for our choice of test where appropriate.

3 What Are the Strongest Emotion–Colour Associations Overall, and How Do Word–Colour Associations Vary According to Linguistic Background?

3.1 Introduction

In this section we answer the first research question in our study:

RQ1: What are the strongest emotion–colour associations overall, and how do word–colour associations vary according to linguistic background?

We present results regarding the most common associations overall and show how the associations varied according to the linguistic backgrounds of the participants. We then look at how the participants with different linguistic backgrounds compared in terms of the colours that they associated with emotions. We show which groups of participants behaved most similarly in this respect and identify interesting cases of variation.

3.2 What Are the Strongest Emotion–Colour Associations Overall?

In order to identify the strongest emotion–colour associations across all participants, we took all 8,520 associations that had been reported and calculated the absolute frequency for each emotion–colour association. In other words, we calculated how often a specific colour (among a selection of twenty-seven) was selected for a given emotion term (fifteen emotion terms overall). As expected, the emotion terms differed significantly from one another in terms of the colours that people associated with them, and the frequencies with which they did so ($\chi^2(364) = 14.214$, p<.001). Table 7 shows the top ten associations, in cases where a colour

Table 7 The ten most common emotion–colour associations (in cases where a colour was selected) in our study

Rank	Emotion term	Colour	N
1	Passionate	Ruby red	244
2	Furious	Ruby red	220
3	Angry	Ruby red	211
4	Happy	Sun yellow	198
5	Cheerful	Sun yellow	195
6	Bored	Grey	189
7	Depressed	Black	154
8	Joyful	Sun yellow	150
9	Calm	Baby blue	132
10	Sad	Grey	124

was selected,[9] across the entire dataset, which includes all five languages.[10]

It is interesting to note that highly intense emotions such as passionate, furious and angry are all associated with the same colour, red, and, moreover, that they are associated with exactly the same shade of red: 'ruby red'. This may indicate that there is a typical red related to these intense emotions across speakers of all six languages, and that the association between red and the emotions passionate, furious and angry might be more widely spread, perhaps reflecting its bodily based nature (we will explore this further in Section 5). Similarly, the same shade of yellow, 'sun yellow', was associated with positive emotion terms such as happy, cheerful and joyful. Again, this association was seen across speakers of all six languages, possibly reflecting the fact that it draws on a widespread inter-action between the body and the natural environment, in that people generally feel happy when the sun is shining (see Section 5).

---

[9] Among the top 10 associations, we also had: Fearful – no association (N = 135) and Confident – no association (N = 125).

[10] Please note that the table shows absolute frequency (i.e. how often a colour was chosen for a given emotion term). The percentages discussed below are based on these absolute frequencies. Since for Italian and Spanish, the number of participants is approximately twice as high as for the other languages, these overall results are slightly skewed towards the most frequent associations in Italian and Spanish.

Two further common associations involve negative but potentially less intense emotions: bored, sad and depressed. These are associated with dark and less saturated colours: black and grey. We will explore the relation between intensity of emotion and saturation of colour, as well as valence of emotion and lightness of colour, in Section 4. The fact that these associations (bored and sad are grey, and depressed is black) surface across speakers of all six languages suggests that there might be a widely shared connection here between intensity of emotion and saturation of colour associated with it, as well as between valence of emotion and lightness of colour associated with it. The strong association between calm and 'baby blue' may be environmentally based given that proximity to the sea induces a sense of calmness in many people, which is reflected in the fact that many meditation practices make use of mental imagery related to the sea or even use the sound of the waves. From these findings, we can conclude that there appears to be a limited number of colour shades that are highly charged with emotional meaning.

In order to investigate this further, we identified the most common colours that were chosen in our study regardless of the emotion term that they were associated with. The findings are shown in Figure 4.

We can see in Figure 4 that the colours 'ruby red' and 'sun yellow' are the two most widely selected colours across the whole dataset. These are followed by

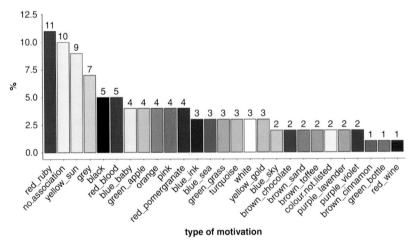

Figure 4 Percentages of colours chosen across all observations (irrespective of emotion term)[11]

---

[11] 'No association' refers to cases where the participants replied that they did not associate the emotion with any particular colour and 'colour not listed' refers to cases where participants replied that the colour with which they associated the emotion could not be found in the list of colours available to them.

grey, 'blood red', and black. In Section 5, we look more deeply into the types of motivations that accompanied these colours in order to investigate whether they are indeed more bodily based, but here we draw the interim conclusion that red (and shades of red), yellow and grey, lend themselves strongly to emotional meaning across speakers of all six languages.

In order to deepen our understanding of the types of colours that participants associated with a specific emotion term, we identified the three most frequent colours that were associated with each of the fifteen emotion terms. The findings are shown in Table 8. The table only reports colours that are significantly more likely to be associated with this emotion than with any other emotion (i.e. that had a residual of 2 or higher, based on the chi-square test reported at the beginning of this section). The figures given in brackets refer to the percentage of cases in which that particular colour was selected for an emotion (this means that '100 per cent' refers to all the colour choices provided for one emotion term (e.g. in 37 per cent of all answers provided for angry, participants chose 'ruby red')).

Again, we see that for the more 'active' emotions (angry, happy, cheerful, excited, passionate, furious and joyful) (see Clarke & Costall, 2008), participants selected bright shades whereas for the more muted emotions (sad, shy, bored and calm), they selected more nuanced shades.

A chi-square test was calculated for the absolute frequency of association across all emotion terms and all colours (i.e. a fifteen by twenty-seven table). In order to get a fuller picture of the colours that were attracted and repelled by the different emotions it is useful to look at the residuals from the chi-square test. Residuals above a value of 2 for a particular emotion–colour association indicate that the association is significantly frequent given the overall distribution of colours chosen for all emotion terms; residuals below a value of -2 indicate that the association is significantly infrequent. To get a clearer picture of the strength of the associations we focus here on the twelve macro categories of colours (findings for the full set of twenty-seven colours are provided in the repository). Even with this reduced set of colours, the chi-square test revealed significant variation between the emotions with respect to the colours that they attracted ($\chi^2(182) = 12{,}342$, p<.001). The residuals from the chi-square test are shown in Figure 5.

As stated at the beginning of this section, the chi-square test and residuals were calculated on the whole data set and not separately for each emotion term. This means that, for example, although 'ruby red' scores fourth highest in absolute frequency among all colour choices for jealous, the association still has a significantly negative residual (i.e. 'ruby red' and jealous are repelled). This is because 'ruby red' scores extremely high frequencies with other emotion terms (e.g. angry, furious, passionate), rendering the overall strength of association with which it was chosen for jealous comparatively small. In Figure 5,

36   *Cognitive Linguistics*

Table 8 The three most common colour associations for each emotion term[12]

Emotion	Most common responses
angry	(ruby red, 37%) (blood red, 22%) (pomegranate red, 12%)
bored	(grey, 34%) (sand brown, 17%) No association (13%) (chocolate brown, 9%)
calm	(baby blue, 23%) (turquoise, 15%) (white 13%)
cheerful	(sun yellow, 35%) (orange, 13%) (gold yellow, 12%)
confident	No association (22%) (sea blue, 11%) (ruby red, 8%)
depressed	(black, 27%) (grey, 20%) (ink blue, 11%)

green tiles indicate that the association was chosen more often than chance would predict (a darker shade of green indicates a higher residual value (i.e. an even more positive association)), red tiles indicate that the association was chosen less often than chance would predict, and grey tiles indicate no

---

[12] For 'sad', both shades of blue and black have the same absolute frequency (N = 69), which is why there are four colours in that row.

Table 8 (cont.)

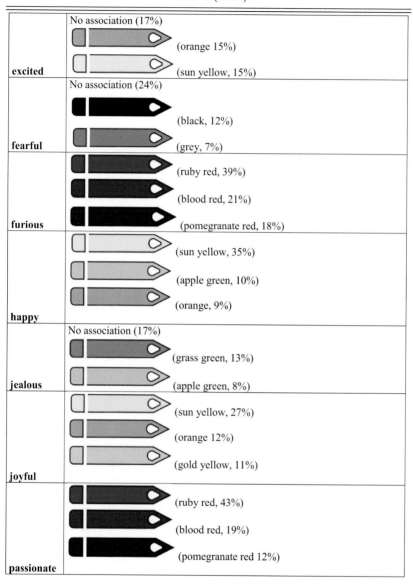

excited	No association (17%)
	(orange 15%)
	(sun yellow, 15%)
fearful	No association (24%)
	(black, 12%)
	(grey, 7%)
furious	(ruby red, 39%)
	(blood red, 21%)
	(pomegranate red, 18%)
happy	(sun yellow, 35%)
	(apple green, 10%)
	(orange, 9%)
jealous	No association (17%)
	(grass green, 13%)
	(apple green, 8%)
joyful	(sun yellow, 27%)
	(orange 12%)
	(gold yellow, 11%)
passionate	(ruby red, 43%)
	(blood red, 19%)
	(pomegranate red 12%)

significant association. The association between angry and red, for example, is particularly strong, as illustrated by the high positive (dark green) residual for the association, but all other possible associations with angry exhibit a significantly low (red) residual. Thus, while angry strongly attracts red it also repels most of the other colours, which in turn strengthens the association between angry and red.

Table 8 (cont.)

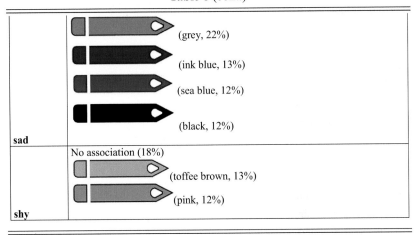

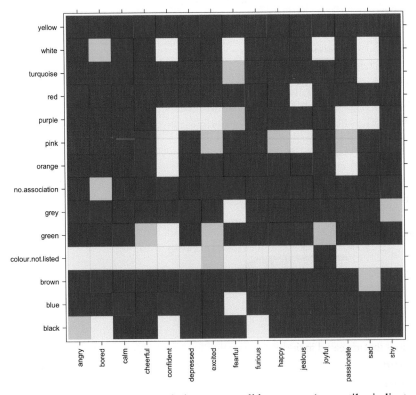

Figure 5 Colour–emotion associations across all languages (green tiles indicate attraction of associations, red tiles indicate repulsion, grey tiles indicate no significant relation).

We can see here that emotions vary considerably in terms of their 'loyalty' to a particular colour. For example, 'furious' is only associated significantly with one colour: red. All the other colours, with the exception of black, are strongly dispreferred. Therefore 'furious' is highly selective in terms of the colours with which it is associated. At the other end of the spectrum, 'shy' associates with a wide range of colours (brown, grey, turquoise, pink, purple and white), and as we will see in Section 5, participants in our study provided a wider range of explanations for their associations for this item. Similarly, the emotion 'bored' is associated with a wider range of colour terms such as white, grey, brown and 'no association'. Unlike the colours that are associated with 'shy', all of these colours have somewhat similar features in that none of them are bright colours. Indeed, brighter colours are strongly repelled for bored. Similarly, the emotion 'calm' is associated with a set of colours that have similar characteristics: white, turquoise, green and blue. This may reflect the fact that nature (green) or the sea (blue) are often associated with a state of calmness. 'Confident' appears to be the emotion term that exhibits the lowest tendency to associate with any colour. Although it was associated with the colour blue, most of the time the choice 'no association' was selected.

In general, the figure shows that just three emotions ('angry', 'passionate' and 'furious') attract strong and consistent colour associations (all with the colour red). For the remaining emotions, participants exhibit a wide range of colour choices, which may reflect the complexity of these emotions or the fact that different options are available, or that there are cross-cultural differences in terms of the colours that are commonly associated with them. It is to this subject that we now turn.

3.3 How Do the Emotion–Colour Associations Vary According to Linguistic Background?

In order to get a picture of how the emotion–colour associations vary across participants with different linguistic backgrounds, it is useful to see what the ten most frequent associations are in each language. These are shown in Table 9a.

In Table 9b, we look again at the ten most common associations overall and show what ranking they had in the responses provided by speakers of each of the different languages. This allows us to compare speakers of different languages and to gain insights into the extent to which each of the different language groups contributed to the overall ranking. Table 9b also shows emotion–colour associations that appeared in the top ten for one of the language groups but not in the top-ten list overall. We have indicated in bold cases where an association that was in the top ten overall received a comparatively low ranking in one of the language groups. For example, the association between depressed and the colour black appears in the top-ten overall list but among the Cantonese participants it received a very low

Table 9a The ten most frequent emotion–colour associations for each language

Rank	American English	British English	Cantonese	German	Italian	Spanish
1	Cheerful is (sun yellow)	Happy is (sun yellow)	Angry is (ruby red)	Passionate is (ruby red)	Passionate is (ruby red)	Furious is (ruby red)
2	Happy is (sun yellow)	Furious is (ruby red)	Passionate is (ruby red)	Bored is (grey)	Bored is (grey)	Passionate is (ruby red)
3	Furious is (ruby red)	Angry is (ruby red)	Furious is (ruby red)	Furious is (ruby red)	Angry is (ruby red)	Sad is (grey)
4	Angry is (ruby red)	Cheerful is (sun yellow)	Shy is (pink)	Jealous is (sun yellow)	Happy is (sun yellow)	Fearful - no association
5	Joyful is (sun yellow)	Joyful is (sun yellow)	Happy is (sun yellow)	Depressed is (black)	Cheerful is (sun yellow)	Bored is (grey)
6	Passionate is (ruby red)	Jealous is (grass green)	Bored is (grey)	Cheerful is (sun yellow)	Sad is (grey)	Cheerful is (sun yellow)
7	Depressed is (black)	Depressed is (black)	Furious is (blood red)	Jealous - no association	Depressed is (black)	Confident - no association
8	Angry is (blood red)	Bored is (grey)	Cheerful is (sun yellow)	Angry is (ruby red)	Furious is (ruby red)	Angry is (ruby red)
9	Sad is (sea blue)	Calm is (baby blue)	Joyful is (sun yellow)	Sad is (black)	Joyful is (sun yellow)	Jealous - no association
10	Calm is (baby blue)	Passionate is (ruby red)	Excited is (ruby red)	Furious is (pomegranate red)	Depressed is (grey)	Depressed is (black)

ranking (fifty-third). Language-specific top-ten ranked associations that deviate from the overall top-ten associations are provided in the lower part of Table 9b.

We can see from Table 9b that the top three associations, furious, angry and passionate, all of which were associated with the same shade of red, are in the top-ten list for speakers of all six languages. This attests to the international salience of these associations. Speakers of all six languages also made associations between cheerful and yellow. For speakers of Cantonese, as we can see in Table 9b, 'depressed' was not frequently associated with black, unlike the other languages. Instead, 'depressed' was more likely to be associated with the colour blue (which is the fifteenth most common association in the Cantonese data). This is interesting because, as we will see in Section 5, associations between depression and blue tend to be culturally based, relating for example to the musical style known as 'the

Table 9b Most frequent emotion–colour associations overall and across languages.

Rank (across languages)	Emotion-colour association	Rank American English	Rank British English	Rank Canton.	Rank German	Rank Italian	Rank Spanish
Top-10 ranked associations (overall) and their ranking in the specific language groups:							
1	Passionate is (ruby red)	6	10	2	1	1	2
2	Furious is (ruby red)	3	2	3	3	8	1
3	Angry is (ruby red)	4	3	1	8	3	8
4	Happy is (sun yellow)	2	1	5	16	4	12
5	Cheerful is (sun yellow)	1	4	8	6	5	6
6	Bored is (grey)	14	8	6	2	2	5
7	Depressed is (black)	7	7	53	5	7	10
8	Joyful is (sun yellow)	5	5	9	12	9	47
9	Fearful (no association)	15	14	76	13	11	4
10	Calm is (baby blue)	10	9	20	23	15	15

Blues'. In Cantonese, people sometimes use the expression 'blue Monday', to refer to the fact that they find the first day of the working week to be depressing. This relates to the English idiom 'to feel blue'. The fact that Cantonese speakers favour this association may therefore reflect the shared cultural history that Hong Kong has with the UK, rather than any bodily based motivation. The assumption that the association between negative emotions and the colour blue is culturally based is also reflected by the fact that the association between blue and the emotion 'sad' was only very frequent among British participants (where it is the ninth most common association).

It is also interesting to note in Table 9b that 'joyful is yellow' is a highly ranked association for all languages except Spanish. Spanish speakers instead tend to associate joyful with the colour pink (which was the eleventh most common association in the Spanish data). This association may be explained by

Table 9b (cont.)

Language-specific top-10 ranked associations that deviate from the overall top10 associations:							
11	Confident (no association)						7
12	Sad is (grey)					6	3
13	Angry is (blood red)	8					
14	Furious is (blood red)			7			
15	Depressed is (grey)					10	
16	Jealous (no association)				7		9
19	Furious is (pomegranate red)				10		
25	Jealous is (grass green)		6				
33	Sad is (black)				9		
34	Sad is (sea blue)	9					
38	Shy is (pink)			4			
43	Excited is (ruby red)			10			
60	Jealous is (sun yellow)				4		

a particular characteristic of the Spanish word for joyful: 'risueña'. This word, which literally means 'smiley' refers directly to the human face, which may turn pink when one is joyful. Alternatively, it may evoke the colour of the mouth: pink. This may explain why it is associated with the colour pink in Spanish but not in the other languages. We look in more detail at the reasons provided by the participants for associations such as this in Section 5.

To get a fuller picture of the colours that were attracted and repelled by the different emotions in the different languages, it is useful to look at the residuals from the chi-square test for each language. These are shown in Figure 6. Again,

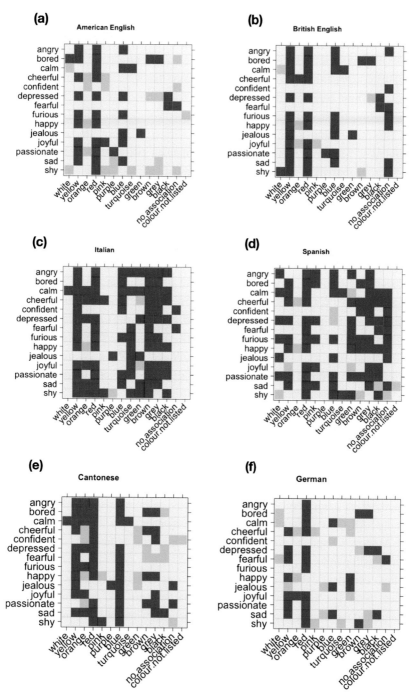

Figure 6 Colour–emotion associations for each language (green tiles indicate attraction of associations, red tiles indicate repulsion, grey tiles indicate no significant relation).

we focus here on the twelve main colours (findings for the full set of twenty-seven colours are provided in the repository).

By looking at the broad patterns in these clusters one can see that the British and American participants reported associations that were largely similar to one another. These are confirmed below, by the table showing the cosine measures (that is, the proximities) between the two varieties of English, which are close to 1. These associations are also somewhat similar to those produced by the Cantonese participants. The Italian and Spanish participants resemble one another in that they appear to favour a small number of associations per emotion, with a large number of associations being actively repelled, as indicated by the preponderance of red tiles in both the Italian and Spanish plots. If we ignore the red tiles and focus only on the green ones, we see that the Spanish and German clusters are somewhat similar to one another.

We can see some interesting differences between the groups of participants in terms of the colours that they associate with particular emotions. Some emotions displayed considerable variation across the groups. For example, 'shy' was strongly associated with just one colour, pink, by the Cantonese-speaking participants, whereas the American English–speaking participants tended to associate it with a much wider range of colours: brown, grey, pink, purple, turquoise and white. The other four groups displayed association patterns that lay at different points between these two extremes.

'Cheerful' was associated with orange and yellow by five of the groups, but some groups (Italian, American and German) also showed strong associations with pink, and others (Spanish, Cantonese and German) associated it with the colour green. A similar pattern was observed for the near-synonym 'happy'. It is interesting that the British English–speaking participants had such a narrow repertoire of associations for these emotions, in comparison with the other groups. All groups tended to associate 'passionate' with the colour red, but the American English– and British English–speaking participants also associated it with purple.

For 'confident', there was a tendency to associate this emotion with the colour blue, but the Cantonese-speaking participants also associated it with orange and the American participants associated it with pink. This might imply that for British, Spanish, Italian and German participants, confidence is a relatively 'inward-facing' emotion, perhaps connoting the idea of being 'quietly confident', whereas for American and Cantonese participants it is a more 'outward-facing' emotion.

For the emotions 'angry' and 'furious', we can see that five of the groups of participants (British, American, Spanish, German and Cantonese) showed strong associations only with the colour red. Interestingly, Italian-speaking participants also tended to associate this emotion with the colour black, suggesting that for Italian speakers, 'angry' may be a darker emotion than for speakers of the other languages. This could be also motivated by the idiomatic expression 'nero di rabbia' (literally, 'black with anger').

'Excited' tended to be associated with colours such as orange, red and pink but Spanish and Italian participants also associated it with the colour green. Most groups associated the emotion 'fearful' with the colour black or brown, but the Germans associated it with white, and the Cantonese associated it with blue. The emotion 'jealous' also exhibited a degree of variation across the groups. Five of the groups (British, American, Italian, Cantonese and German) tended to associate it with the colour green but some groups (Italian, German and Cantonese) also associated it with the colour purple, one group (Germans) associated it with the colour yellow, and one group (Spanish) showed no strong associations with any particular colour. A potential reason for the heterogeneity among German-speaking participants regarding colour choices for 'jealous' may be explained by the fact that participants were shown two different terms for that emotion, *eifersüchtig* and *neidisch*, the latter of which being closer to English 'envious'. Responses for both terms were collapsed into one category for the sake of comparison. A close analysis of the data reveals that *eifersüchtig* ('to be jealous of someone you love') is more often associated with red due to its conceptual overlap with angry or passionate. *Neidisch* ('jealous of something that someone else has or can do') is more often associated with green or yellow due to the idiomatic expression 'grün vor Neid' ('green with envy') and folk anatomy associating jealousy with yellow bile.

Other emotions displayed very little variation across the different groups. For the emotion 'bored', participants from all six language backgrounds tended to display the same behaviour in terms of their associations, with all six groups selecting brown and grey, and one or two selecting other unsaturated colours, black and white. Similarly, for 'calm', participants from all backgrounds chose blue and turquoise. Finally, all six groups tended to associate 'sad' with blue, and four of them associated 'depressed' with blue, which suggests that the idea of 'the blues' representing sadness is widespread. Participants from all six backgrounds associated both 'sad' and 'depressed' with unsaturated colours such as brown, black and grey, but the Cantonese participants also tended to associate the colour purple with depressed.

Although Figure 6 tells us a good deal about what kinds of colours tended to be associated with different emotions in the different languages at the level of the individual emotions, it does not tell us how similar the languages were to one another in terms of their overall emotion–colour associations. In order to find this out, we constructed a contingency matrix in which the six languages were displayed on the columns, and all the emotion–colour associations produced by all the speakers were displayed on the rows. In the intersecting cells we reported the frequency by which speakers of a given language indicated that association. For example, for the association between bored and grey we observed nineteen occurrences produced by American participants, twenty-six occurrences produced by British participants, fifty-six occurrences produced by Italian participants, twenty-five occurrences produced by Cantonese participants, twenty-seven occurrences produced by German participants and thirty-seven occurrences produced by Spanish participants.

Once the contingency matrix had been filled, we normalised the raw frequencies because the total amount of judgements collected for each language was not the same across languages, as languages that mark grammatical gender had roughly twice the number of participants. We then obtained a numeric vector that represented each language in terms of its distribution of emotion–colour associations. Then, we computed the geometric distance between each pair of languages (each pair of vectors), using the 'lsa' package in R (Wild, 2020). As in classic distributional semantic studies, the distance was calculated using the formula for the cosine, which measures the geometrical proximity between two vectors. The cosine measure, which ranges from −1 to 1, is somewhat similar to correlation coefficients (but for a discussion of the differences between the two metrics, see Bolognesi, 2020). We obtained the table of relative distances between each two languages (see Table 10). On the diagonal, the maximum value (cosine =1) is reported, because this represents the proximity between a language and itself. In the rest of the cells, the higher the value, the closer the patterns of emotion–colour associations found in the two languages.

Table 10 Cosine similarities showing the extent to which the different languages relate to one another in terms of their pattern distributions of emotion–colour associations.

	American English	British English	Italian	Spanish	Cantonese	German
American English	1.00	0.91	0.79	0.80	0.72	0.76
British English	0.91	1.00	0.80	0.78	0.72	0.75
Italian	0.79	0.80	1.00	0.85	0.77	0.85
Spanish	0.80	0.78	0.85	1.00	0.74	0.80
Cantonese	0.72	0.72	0.77	0.74	1.00	0.71
German	0.76	0.75	0.85	0.80	0.71	1.00

Looking at this table, we see that the responses provided by the American English speakers display a very high cosine measure (cos = 0.91) with those provided by the British English speakers. This means that the overall, emotion–colour associations provided by these two groups are very similar to one another. The responses provided by the American English speakers also display similar patterns of associations to those provided by the Spanish, German and Italian speakers (cosines between 0.80 and 0.76). Finally, the responses that are most distant to those provided by the American English speakers are those provided by the Cantonese speakers. These patterns of similarities and differences seem to reflect to some extent the geographical distances between the places where the participants lived. Looking at British English, we observe a very similar behaviour compared to what was already reported for American English. Italian speakers show more similar patterns of associations to Spanish and German speakers (Cos = 0.85) than with British and American English speakers and finally with Cantonese. Similar observations can be derived for the other languages. Overall, Cantonese shows a patterns of colour–emotion associations that is the most different (lower cosines) from the other languages. This is intuitively understandable since the Cantonese language is a non-Indo-European language, and therefore different both typologically and genealogically from the other (European) languages in the sample.

Plotting the similarities between languages on two dimensions, after a multi-dimensional scaling analysis (package 'stats', R core team), we obtain the map displayed in Figure 7, which summarises on a bidimensional plan the similarities between patterns of associations across languages.

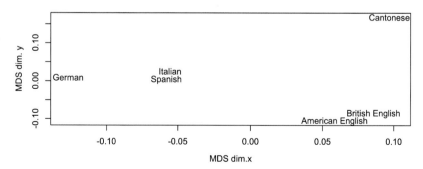

Figure 7 Multidimensional scaling (MDS) analysis displayed in a two-dimensional plot, showing the proximities between the language vectors, reflecting the similarities in patterns of emotion–colour associations provided by the speakers.

3.4 Conclusion

In this section, we have explored emotion–colour associations in general and across languages. What is interesting to see is that very intense emotions such as passionate, furious and angry are all associated with the same colour, red, and in fact even with the same shade of red, 'ruby red'. This may indicate that there is a 'typical' red related to these intense emotions across all six languages considered. In Section 5, we explore the extent to which this association is bodily based. Similarly, the same shade of yellow, 'sun yellow', is associated with positive emotions terms such as happy, cheerful and joyful. Again, this association emerges across all six languages, and in Section 5 we explore the idea that it may be bodily or environmentally motivated. Two further common associations are the two negative but potentially less intense emotions of bored and depressed, which are associated with dark and less saturated colours such as black and grey. We will explore the relation between intensity of emotion and saturation of colour, as well as valence of emotion and lightness of colour in Section 4. The fact that these associations (bored is grey and depressed is black) surface across all six languages suggests that there might be a widespread connection between intensity of emotion and saturation of colour associated with it, as well as between valence of emotion and lightness of colour associated with it.

In terms of linguistic variation, we observed very strong similarities between the associations provided by the British and American English participants, which was expected. We also observed that Cantonese, the language that is most typologically and geographically distant from the other languages in the sample, shows patterns of emotion–colour associations that are less similar to any of the other languages, on average, suggesting that the typological and geographical distance of this language from the other languages in our study is reflected in the array of emotion–colour associations provided by its speakers.

4 How Do Emotional Valence and Intensity Map onto Colour Lightness and Saturation, and How Do These Relationships Vary According to the Linguistic Background of the Participants and the Gender of the Prompt?

4.1 Introduction

So far in this Element we have examined the associations that are formed between particular emotions and particular colours and have identified some associations that appear to be more widespread and others that are more susceptible to cross-linguistic/cross-cultural variation. In this section, we turn our attention to the individual properties of the emotions and the colours. We explore the metaphorical relationship between the valence and the intensity of the emotions and the lightness and saturation of the colours. In so doing, we address the second research question in our study:

RQ2 How do emotional valence and intensity map onto colour lightness and saturation, and how do these relationships vary according to linguistic background?

In order to answer this research question, we used normed data for both intensity and valence for each of the emotions to investigate whether there are any relationships between these norms and the saturation and lightness of the colours that people associate with them.

Saturation refers to the brilliance or strength of a colour. As saturation increases, colours appear more 'pure'. As saturation decreases, colours appear more 'washed-out'. The saturation of a colour can be reduced by adding shades of grey. In turn, lightness refers to the relative lightness or darkness of a particular colour, from black (which contains no lightness) to white (which contains full lightness). Figure 8 shows different degrees of saturation and lightness of the colour red.

We saw in Section 1 that there is some research suggesting that emotions involving higher levels of intensity are more likely to be related to strongly

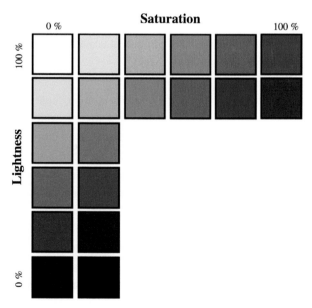

Figure 8 Degrees of saturation and lightness for the colour red[13]

[13] Source: Adapted from https://commons.wikimedia.org/wiki/File:Saturation_and_Value_(2).png

saturated colours. This kind of relationship would reflect a metaphorical mapping of intensity across the two domains. Previous research into cross-modal mappings has found that intensity is one of the main drivers of such mappings, for example, Slobodenyuk, Jraissati, Kanso, Ghanem & Elhajj (2015) found that the intensity of haptic stimuli are reflected in the colours that correspond to them. Therefore, in our study, we expected to find a positive correlation between the intensity of the emotion and the degree of saturation of the colours with which it was associated.

According to conceptual metaphor theory, in many cultures, there is a strong relationship between light colours and positive emotions. This relationship has been found to manifest in a wide variety of forms of expression ranging from language (Lakoff & Johnson, 1980) to feature films, where light is often associated with positivity and darkness is associated with negativity (Forceville & Renckens, 2013). There is evidence to suggest that these associations are mentally represented implicitly and automatically (Meier & Robinson, 2005; Meier et al., 2007). Therefore, in our study, we expected to find a positive correlation between the valence of the emotion and the lightness of the colours with which it was associated. The idea that intensity and positive-negative valence of emotions are two of the main driving forces for cross-modal mappings is also supported by findings from studies that have identified cross-modal correspondences between colours and smells (Gilbert, Martin & Kemp, 1996; Schifferstein & Tanudjaja, 2004), colours and tastes (Spence et al., 2010), and colours and sounds (Palmer et al., 2013).

At this point, it is useful to consider how and why associations between valence and lightness and between intensity and saturation might have arisen. In Section 1, we discussed a range of mechanisms through which people form associations between emotions and colours, ranging from bodily based experiences through to language and interaction with the environment. We also saw that some associations appear to be 'hard-wired' into the brain. Here we consider how each of these acquisition mechanisms might account for the ways in which people develop associations between intensity and saturation and between valence and lightness. We also consider how these different acquisition mechanisms might account for any cross-cultural variation that is encountered.

We begin by discussing how the acquisition mechanisms outlined in Section 1 might contribute to the relationship between valence and lightness. The idea that positive things tend to be seen as 'light' and negative things tend to be seen as 'dark' is widespread and manifests in a wide variety of the world's languages. This relationship appears to have a bodily based motivation, as humans respond positively to sunlight given that it allows them to go about their daily business.

Similarly, the experience of darkness has been found to provoke negative emotional states, including fear or anxiety (Grillon, Pellowski, Merikangas & Davis, 1997), and is therefore more negative. The widespread nature of the relationship between goodness and light (and badness and darkness), along with the fact that the relationship appears to go beyond language, has led some to describe it as a 'conceptual metaphor' (i.e. a metaphor that exists not just in language, but also in thought; Lakoff and Johnson, 1980). According to conceptual metaphor theory, the 'source domain' DEGREE OF LIGHT represents the 'target domain' DEGREE OF GOODNESS at the level of both language and thought.

There may however be some variation in the universality of this metaphor. There may, for example, be some types of environmental variation that shape the extent to which lightness is associated with positive emotions. For example, citizens of countries that are less exposed to sunlight throughout the year, may develop a more positive association between light and positive emotions. The relationship between lightness and valence is also likely to be shaped by exposure to the linguistic environment. These differences may also lead to variation in the extent to which the two phenomena are related. In other words, the linguistic conventions may lead to variations in the strength of the associations that people form between valence and lightness. Another possibility is that the emotions themselves may be viewed differently by members of the different cultural groups. This would affect the overall levels of lightness of the colours that people associate with them. There may also be cultural differences in the ways in which colours are used, and the kinds of colours that people are habitually exposed to. This may also affect overall preferences in terms of the lightness of the colours that are selected.

The relationship between intensity and saturation is somewhat different in kind to the relationship between valence and lightness. While GOOD IS LIGHT is a widely discussed conceptual metaphor, the relationship between intensity and saturation is more a question of degree (in this case more feeling = more saturation), a property that can be mapped from the source domain to the target domain, regardless of the conceptual metaphor involved. This idea is encapsulated in Barnden and colleagues' (2003) 'vehicle neutral mapping adjuncts' (VNMAs). Rather than taking an interest in individual metaphors, Barnden and colleagues argue that there are a number of properties, attributes, relations and qualities, such as 'qualitative degree', 'causation' and others, that cut across the conventional division of metaphors into families organised around a conceptual metaphor. This suggests that the relationship between emotional intensity and colour saturation may be more fundamental than the relationship between emotional valence and colour lightness, and that it might therefore be less susceptible to cross-cultural variation.

To probe these issues in depth, in our study, we explored the similarities and differences in the responses provided by the British English–, American English–, Spanish-, Italian-, German- and Cantonese-speaking participants in our study. More specifically we were interested to see whether any of these groups chose lighter/darker or more or less saturated colours across the board. In terms of the relationships between valence and lightness and between intensity and saturation, we first established whether such relationships existed in general. We then investigated whether the relationships were equally strong in all groups of participants or whether there were some groups of participants who exhibited unusually strong or unusually weak relationships in comparison with the other groups.

4.2 Findings

The specific research questions that we explore in this section are:

1. Does the valence of the emotion relate to the lightness of the colours that are associated with it, and if so, does this vary according to the linguistic background of the participants?
2. does the intensity of the emotion relate to the saturation of the colours that are associated with it, and if so, does this vary according to the linguistic background of the participants? Here we discuss our findings in relation to these two questions.

4.2.1 Does Emotional Valence Relate to Colour Lightness?

We began by investigating whether positive words were more likely to be associated with lighter colours (and negative words with darker colours). Valence and intensity were operationalised using the data described in Section 2. We found this to be the case: there was a moderate positive correlation between how positive a word was (i.e. its valence) and the lightness of the colours that were associated with it ($r = 0.48$, p<.001; estimate: 4.48, standard error (SE) = 0.87; p<.001).

Besides providing p-values, when we report the results of our mixed linear regression models, if the relationship turns out to be significant (i.e. p<.05), we additionally provide the estimate to explain the relationship between the predictor and the outcome, as well as the SE. What the estimate tells us is how many units in the y axis is expected from a change of unit in the x axis. For example, our estimate of 4.48 predicts that words with a rating of 4 in valence are likely to be associated with colours that are lighter by 4.48 per cent than words with a valence score of 3; and consequently, words scoring 5 in valence are 4.48 per cent lighter than valence ratings of 4, and so on. In other words, the estimate gives as an approximate idea of the strength of the effect of emotional valence on colour lightness.

In addition to this, the estimate can help us to predict the exact lightness value of the different words. If words scoring 3 for valence have an associated colour lightness value of approximately 60 per cent, the estimate tells us that words with a valence rating of 4 would have an associated colour lightness value of approximately 64.5 per cent (60% + 4.48%). Finally, we also report the adjusted R^2 value of the model (AdjR^2). This measure gives us an idea of the strength of the predictor in terms of its ability to explain variation in the data, as it explains how much variation in the data can be explained by the model in question. In this case, this is 22 per cent, which is fairly high. The findings are shown in Figure 9.

These findings show that there was a significant relationship between the valence of an emotion and the lightness of the colours that participants associated with it, across the board, in that more positive emotion terms were associated with lighter (shades of) colours. This finding is consistent with previous work in this area.

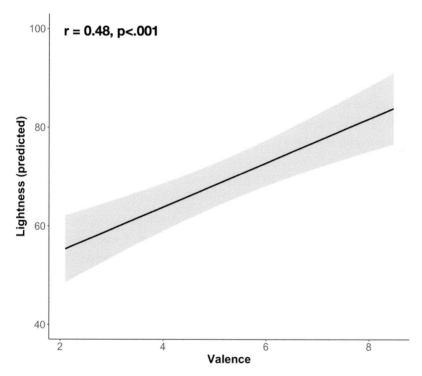

Figure 9 Overall relationship between valence and lightness

Cognitive Linguistics

Table 11 Emotions with the lowest, middle and highest valence scores, and their associated colours

Valence (lowest, middle and highest value)	Lightness (average)	Lightness values for the most commonly associated colours
2.27 ('depressed')	38.80%	(black, 11%) (grey, 56%)
5.16 ('shy')	75.23%	(toffee brown, 88%) (pink, 90%)
8.21('joyful')	86.05%	(sun yellow, 92%), (orange, 89%)

To unpack this finding, it is useful to look at the emotions that had the lowest, middle and highest valence scores and to see what kinds of colours they were associated with. These are shown in Table 11. As we can see in this table, the emotions with the lowest and highest valences respectively (depressed and joyful) have very clear associations with dark colours (black and grey) and light colours (yellow and orange) respectively. This reflects the idea that GOOD IS LIGHT and BAD IS DARK that has been discussed extensively in the literature on conceptual metaphor (Lakoff, 1993; Lakoff & Johnson, 1980). The colours that are associated with 'shy' are more mixed. As we will see in Section 5, when providing reasons for associations involving the colour brown participants often made reference to the nature of the colour itself, whereas for pink, they were more likely to make metonymic references to the fact that our cheeks turn pink when we feel shy. These mixed motivations may explain why terms such as this, that do not have a single, clear association are found more in the middle of the values provided in Table 11.

4.2.2 Does the Relationship Between Emotional Valence and Colour Lightness Vary According to Linguistic Background?

Our correlational analyses showed that the relationship between the valence of the emotion and lightness of the colour with which it was associated was susceptible to variation across the different linguistic backgrounds. To calculate this, we built a mixed linear model where we introduced 'Valence' as predictor in interaction with 'Linguistic Background', and 'Lightness' as outcome. 'Participant' and 'Item' were also introduced as random effects. The different patterns are shown in Figure 10.

The first observation to make is that British participants were more likely to choose lighter colours than all other participants, significantly more than the American ($p<.01$), German ($p<.001$), Italian ($p<.001$) and Spanish participants

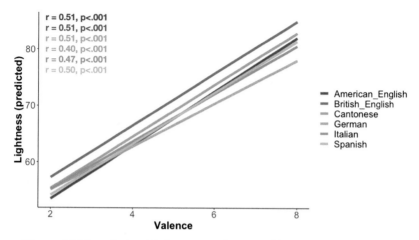

Figure 10 The relationship between valence and lightness across the six linguistic backgrounds

(p<.001). The Cantonese participants responded in a similar way to the British participants (p = .52), although they tended to choose slightly darker colours.

We can also see in Figure 10 that the line representing the responses provided by the American participants is much steeper than the lines representing the responses produced by participants from the other cultural backgrounds. Indeed, the line representing the responses provided by the American partici-pants was significantly steeper than the lines representing the responses of the German (p<.01) and Italian (p<.05) participants. This means that the colour choices (in terms of lightness) of the responses produced by the American participants were much more sensitive to valence than those made by partici-pants from other backgrounds. In other words, the American participants chose darker colours for sadder words, and comparatively lighter colours for happier words.

To illustrate what this means, let us look at how the American responses to a positive emotion (happy) and a negative emotion (depressed) compared with the responses provided by participants from different cultural backgrounds. Figure 11 takes these two emotions and shows how the responses of the American participants compared with those of the German, Italian and Spanish participants.

We see in Figure 11 that for the word 'happy' (a positively valenced word), the American participants were more likely to choose a lighter shade of yellow than their German, Italian and Spanish counterparts. Conversely, for the word 'depressed' (a negatively valenced word) they were more likely to choose a

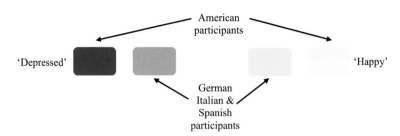

Figure 11 An illustration showing the heightened response patterns of the Americans in comparison to three other cultural groups: darker colours associated with negative emotions and lighter colours associated with positive emotions

darker shade of blue than their German, Italian and Spanish counterparts. In other words, in comparison to other participants, the American participants made fuller use of the whole lightness spectrum, selecting shades from the extremities of the spectrum. The difference is particularly marked at the lower end of the spectrum. Here the line representing the responses provided by the American participants is lower than those representing all the responses of all the other participants. This indicates that American participants were more likely than all other participants to choose darker colours when presented with negative emotions.

In contrast, the German participants showed the opposite tendency. The line representing responses by the German participants has the least steep gradient, indicating that the correlation between valence and lightness was least pronounced in German participants (while still being statistically significant; $r = 0.40$, $p<.001$). The German participants also tended to choose darker colours for happy emotions compared to the other language. Thus, the German participants in our study appeared to be avoiding extremes in both cases.

4.2.3 Does the Relationship between Emotional Valence and Colour Lightness Vary According to the Gender of the Prompt?

We saw in Section 1 that people tend to associate light colours with women and dark colours with men, so here we ask: are emotions more likely to be associated with lighter colours when they appear in the feminine form? In other words, will the feminine form of the word *furiosa* ('furious' in English) attract lighter colours than its masculine equivalent *furioso*?

The mean scores and distributions for masculine and feminine prompts in terms of the overall lightness of the colours with which they were associated are shown in Figure 12 (Spanish and Italian data only since only those exhibit a gender distinction for the emotion adjective).

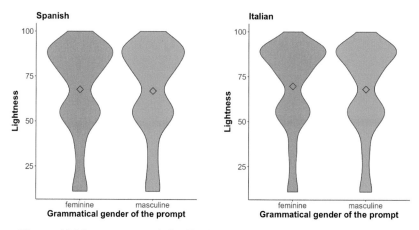

Figure 12 Mean scores and distributions of the overall lightness ratings of colours associated with masculine and feminine prompts

No significant differences were found between the two kinds of prompt in this respect: in both Spanish and Italian masculine and feminine prompts tended to be associated with colours that had similar lightness ratings. In the Spanish data, the average lightness value for feminine adjectives was 69 per cent, while for masculine adjectives it was 68 per cent. In the Italian data, the average lightness value for feminine adjectives was 70 per cent, while for masculine adjectives it was 68 per cent.

Next, we explored whether the extent to which valence maps onto lightness varies according to the gender of the prompt. Here we found no significant interactions for the Spanish prompts but we did find a significant effect in the Italian data (p<.05, AdjR^2 = 0.36). This suggests that there was a small but significant tendency in the Italian participants to rate feminine adjectives with lighter colours in response to their valence, particularly at the lower end of the valence scale. The findings are shown in Figure 13.

It is interesting to note in Figure 13 that the difference between masculine and feminine prompts that was found in the Italian data is much more marked at the 'low valence' end of the scale than at the 'high valence' end of the scale. This means that differences in terms of the way gendered nouns are perceived in Italian are more noticeable for negatively valenced emotions than for positively valenced emotions. To illustrate this, let us take the negatively valenced emotion 'depressed' (which had a valence score of 2.27). As shown in Figure 14, we found that that the mean lightness score of colours that were associated with the feminine form *depressa* (16.41) was lighter than the mean lightness score of

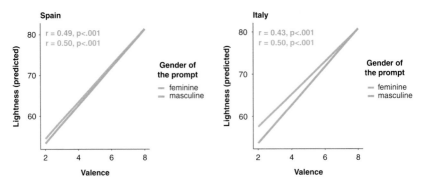

Figure 13 Associations between the valence of the emotion and the lightness of the colours with which it was associated for masculine and feminine prompts (in Spanish and Italian)

colours that were associated with the masculine form *depresso* (15.2). The percentages or colour choices associated with the feminine form *depressa* and the masculine form *depresso* are shown in Figure 13. Colours are ordered in increasing order of lightness: black (11%), brown (chocolate) (22%), green (bottle) (31%), blue (ink) (34%), red (wine) (39%), brown (sand) (46), purple (violet) (52%), grey (56%), blue (sea) (58%), turquoise (62%), brown (cinnamon) (63%), purple (lavender) (75%), blue (sky) (77%), brown (toffee) (88%), and blue (baby) (93%).

We can see from Figure 14 that black and grey were the most frequent choices for both *depressa* and *depresso*. However, they were more strongly associated with the masculine form *depresso* (black: 28%; grey: 26%) than with the feminine form *depressa* (black: 25%; grey: 24%). For the feminine form *depressa*, there was greater use of lighter colours such as blue (ink) (10%; 0% for the masculine version) and violet (6%; only 1% for the masculine version). Participants were also more likely to give 'no association' for masculine *depresso* than for feminine *depressa*. Here we see gender stereotypes coming into play as feminine depression is seen as less 'dark', more colourful and somehow 'prettier' than masculine depression. Or, in other words, feminine depression may be seen as less dark and therefore in a way less intense than masculine depression. There is indirect evidence of metonymic thinking in this finding as it suggests that people associate the emotion with the person experiencing the emotion before deciding what kind of emotion it is. These gendered perceptions of depression are interesting as they may have implications for how people think about men and women when they are depressed. More extensive research would be required to assess whether this is indeed the case.

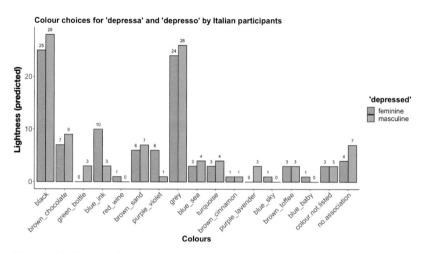

Figure 14 Colours that Italian participants associated with feminine *depressa* and masculine *depresso* expressed in percentages with their corresponding lightness values.

4.2.4 Does Emotional Intensity Relate to Colour Saturation?

We also investigated whether emotions that have higher intensity ratings were more likely to be associated with more saturated colours. As predicted, our correlational analyses showed a significant relationship between intensity and saturation ($r = 0.46$, $p<.001$; estimate of intensity ratings: 10.14, SE = 2.34, $p<.001$). This model accounted for 20 per cent of the variation in the colour associations (AdjR^2 = 0.20). The findings are shown in Figure 15.

These findings show that there was a significant relationship between the intensity of an emotion and the degree of saturation of the colours that participants associated with it, across the board. This finding is also consistent with previous work in this area.

To unpack this finding, it is useful to look at the emotions that had the lowest, middle and highest intensity scores and to see what kinds of colours they were associated with. These are shown in Table 12. As we can see in this table, the emotions with the lowest and highest intensity levels (calm and excited) have very clear associations with unsaturated ('baby blue', turquoise and white) and highly saturated colours ('sun yellow' and orange) respectively. The colours associated with 'calm' appear to reflect bodily interactions with the environment, perhaps drawing on ideas related to the sea and the sky. The same can be said for the colours that are associated with 'excited', as they may relate to the notion of heat. In contrast, the emotions associated with

Table 12 Emotions with the lowest, middle and highest intensity scores, and their associated colours

Intensity (lowest, middle and highest value)	Saturation (average)	Most common colours associated with these emotions and their saturation levels
1.67 (e.g., 'calm')	45.70%	(baby blue, 49%) (turquoise, 35%) (white 0%)
4.62 (e.g., 'confident')	61.96%	(sea blue, 85%) (ruby red, 93%)
6.43 ('excited')	73.10%	(sun yellow, 80%) (orange, 85%)

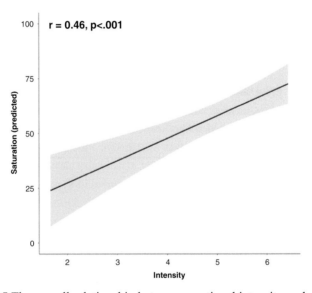

r = 0.46, p<.001

Saturation (predicted) vs *Intensity*

Figure 15 The overall relationship between emotional intensity and saturation

'confident' are more mixed. As we saw in our discussion of the relationship between valence and lightness, mixed motivations may explain why terms such as 'confident' are found more in the middle of the table. We examine the exact motivations of these responses in more depth in Section 5. For now, it suffices to say that for both valence and lightness and for intensity and saturation it appears to be the case that there is more agreement between participants on the types of colours that are associated with emotions that lie towards the ends of the positive/negative and the high/low intensity continuum; whereas for emotions that lie in the middle of the continua, competing motivations appear to come into play.

4.2.5 Does the Relationship between Emotional Intensity and Colour Saturation Vary According to Linguistic Background?

To explore this question, we entered in our mixed linear model 'Intensity' as predictor in interaction with 'Linguistic Background' and 'Saturation' as outcome. As we did for our analysis of valence, we also added 'Participant' and 'Item' as random effects. Our findings showed that the relationship between the intensity of the emotion and degree of saturation of the colour with which it was associated was susceptible to variation across the speakers of different languages. The different patterns are shown in Figure 16.

On balance, the Cantonese-, the British English– and the American English–speaking participants tended to choose more saturated colours than the participants from the other linguistic backgrounds (p<.001), whereas the Spanish (p<.01) and Italian (p<.001) participants tended to choose the least saturated colours.

Interestingly however, in contrast to our findings concerning the relationship between valence and lightness, the relationship between intensity and saturation was weakest in the American participants. In other words, the gradient of the slope showing the responses of the American participants is much less steep than those for the participants from the other cultural backgrounds. This suggests that the Americans were more likely to choose more saturated colours on

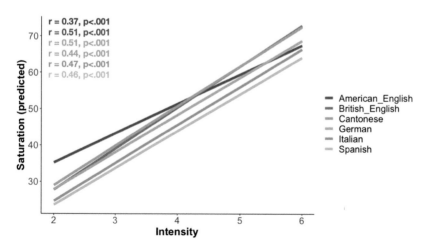

Figure 16 The relationship between intensity and saturation across the six linguistic backgrounds

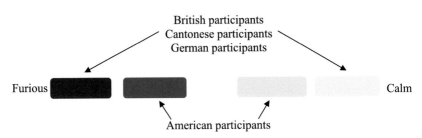

Figure 17 An illustration showing the less extreme response patterns of the Americans in comparison to three other cultural groups: colours associated with intense emotions are on average less saturated (dull, muted) while colours associated with non-intense emotions are more saturated (with less grey).

average for emotions that were low in intensity (feelings like 'calm') than the British, Cantonese and German participants; and, conversely, less saturated colours for feelings high in intensity (e.g. 'furious') than their British, Cantonese and German counterparts. To illustrate what this means, let us look at how the responses provided by the American participants to a high-intensity emotion (furious) and a low-intensity emotion (calm) compared with the responses provided by participants from three other linguistic backgrounds. Figure 17 takes these two emotions and shows how the responses of the American participants compared with those of the British, Cantonese and German participants.

We see in Figure 16 that for the word 'furious' (a 'high-intensity' word), the American participants were likely to choose a less saturated shade of red than their British, Cantonese and German counterparts. Conversely, for the word 'calm' (a 'low-intensity' word), they were more likely to choose a more saturated shade of blue than their British, Cantonese and German counterparts. In other words, in comparison to other participants, the American participants made less use of the whole saturation spectrum, avoiding shades from the extremities of the spectrum. The difference is particularly marked at the lower end of the spectrum. Here the line representing the responses provided by the American participants is higher than those representing the responses of all the other participants. This indicates that the American participants were less likely than participants with other linguistic backgrounds to choose saturated colours when presented with high intensity emotions. It is interesting to compare this finding to the finding that we made regarding the relationship between valence and lightness. Whereas American participants appear to be highly sensitive to valence, in expressing their associations between colours and emotions, especially negative valence, they appear to be much less sensitive than the participants from other linguistic backgrounds to intensity, in this specific task. It is somewhat difficult to explain this finding. One explanation may relate to relatively high levels of extraversion in US citizens in comparison with other nationalities (Lynn & Martin, 1995); high levels of extraversion have been found to relate to a reduced sensitivity to the arousing properties of emotions (Kehoe et al., 2012).

4.2.6 Does the Relationship between Emotional Intensity and Colour Saturation Vary According to the Gender of the Prompt?

In Section 1, we saw that in many cultures women are expected to experience, and to express, more 'muted' emotions than men. Men's emotions in contrast are expected to be more 'intense'. This leads us to ask whether emotions are more likely to be associated with more saturated colours when they appear in the masculine form. In other words, will an emotion such as *furiosa/o* be associated with more saturated colours when it appears in its masculine form (*furioso*) than when it appears in its feminine form (*furiosa*)? The mean scores and distributions for the degree of saturation selected for the different prompts in our Spanish and Italian participants are shown in Figure 18.

There were no significant differences between the mean saturation values of the colours selected for masculine prompts and for feminine prompts in either Spanish (mean saturation value for feminine prompts: 53%; mean saturation value for masculine prompts: 55%) or Italian (mean saturation value for feminine prompts: 56%; mean saturation value for colours associated with masculine prompts: 55%).

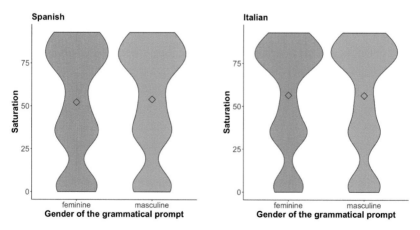

Figure 18 Mean scores and distributions of saturation values of the colours selected for masculine and feminine prompts in Spanish and Italian

Cognitive Linguistics

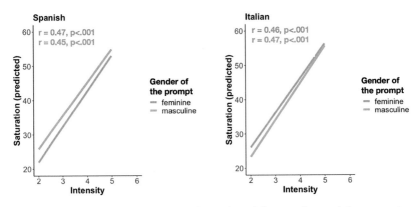

Figure 19 Associations between the intensity of the emotion and the saturation levels of the colours with which it was associated for masculine and feminine prompts (in Spanish and Italian)

We then looked at the extent to which intensity of an emotion served as a predictor for saturation, in order to see whether there are differences between the choices made for masculine and feminine adjectives in this respect. In other words, we compared the respective gradients of the slopes for the masculine and feminine prompts in both Spanish and Italian. These are shown in Figure 19.

Here we found no significant interactions for the Spanish prompts ($p = .48$) or for the Italian prompts ($p = .76$). In other words, saturation is not more strongly related to intensity in either the masculine or the feminine prompts.

4.3 Conclusion

In this section, we have seen that the valence of an emotion is metaphorically related to the lightness of the colour that it is associated with; that is to say, more positive emotions tend to be associated with lighter colours and more negative emotions are associated with darker colours. More intense emotions tend to be associated with more saturated colours, and less intense emotions tend to be associated with less saturated colours. Both of these findings were highly significant across the board. However, there were cross-cultural differences both in terms of the overall levels of lightness and saturation and in terms of the degree to which these properties were associated.

In terms of the lightness of the colours selected, British and Cantonese participants tended to choose colours that were lighter overall in comparison with the other participants, regardless of the emotions with which they were associated. There are two ways to interpret this finding. Firstly, it could be that these groups perceive the emotions in a more positive light than the other participants, or it could simply be that they prefer lighter colours more generally. The fact that British and Cantonese participants pattern together in this respect may reflect their shared cultural history, as we have already discussed. In terms of the relationship between the valence of the emotion and the lightness of the colours with which it was associated, American participants were significantly more sensitive than participants with other linguistic backgrounds.

As for saturation, Spanish and Italian participants tended to select colours that were less saturated overall, in comparison with the other participants. In terms of the relationship between the intensity of the emotion and the degree of saturation of the colours with which it was associated, American participants were significantly *less* sensitive than participants with other linguistic backgrounds. It is interesting to observe this reverse patterning in the American participants. They appear to be much more sensitive to valence than to intensity, when asked to associate emotions with colours. This finding may relate to levels of extraversion in the American participants, but further research would be required to confirm or disconfirm this link.

When we looked at the gender of the prompt, we saw that masculine adjectives exhibited a stronger relationship between valence and lightness than feminine adjectives. The strongest differences were found at the negative end of the scale, suggesting that when negative emotions are presented, they are more likely to be associated with darker colours when they appear in the masculine form than when they appear in the feminine form. These findings suggest that, for example, male sadness may be considered more 'negative' than female sadness. No differences were found between masculine and feminine adjectives for the relationship between intensity and saturation.

5 What Reasons Do People Provide for Emotion–Colour Associations and How Do These Reasons Vary According to Linguistic Background, the Emotion Being Discussed, and the Colour Being Selected? If an Association is Bodily Related, Is It More Likely to Be Widely Shared?

5.1 Introduction

In this section, we answer the third research question in our study:

RQ3 What reasons do people provide for emotion–colour associations and how do these reasons vary according to linguistic background, the emotion being discussed, and the colour being selected? If an association is bodily related, is it more likely to be widely shared?

By inviting participants to explain the reasons for their emotion–colour associations, we hoped to tap into people's explicit as well as their implicit conceptualisations of emotion terms, and to discover how they vary across different linguistic backgrounds. In this section we therefore explore the reasons or 'motivations' that the participants provided for their choices in response to the open-answer format questions. We begin by looking at the relative numbers of the overall types of motivation provided. We then look at how these differed according to the linguistic backgrounds of the participants, the emotions being discussed and the colours being selected. In the final section, we explore whether bodily based motivations are more widely shared than linguistic and culturally mediated motivations.

5.2 What Are the Most Common Motivations?

The percentages of motivation types chosen by all participants are shown in Figure 20.[14]

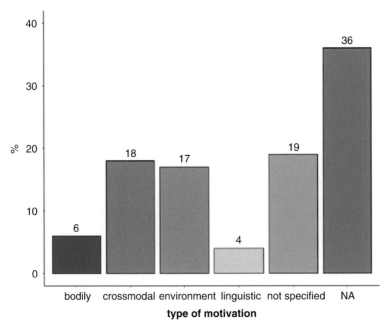

Figure 20 Percentages of motivation types chosen (N = 8,520/100%)

---

[14] It should be emphasised that the numbers shown in this figure include responses provided by all participants. Since we roughly obtained twice as much data from Italian and Spanish participants, the numbers are slightly skewed with respect to these two groups of participants. Still, we believe that the figure provides an interesting first idea of what kinds of motivations were most frequently provided by all our participants.

We can see in Figure 20 that in cases where a motivation was provided (i.e. disregarding the categories 'not specified' and 'NA'), the most common kind of motivation was cross-modal, followed by environmental, then bodily motivated, then linguistic. It should be noted at this point that this ordering does not represent any overall 'universal' ordering that people might have for selecting a type of motivation. If we had included a different set of emotions in our study, we may well have seen a different pattern of responses. However, they do serve as a baseline against which we can study the ways in which motivations varied according to the linguistic background of the participants, the emotion being considered and the colour that it was being associated with. It is therefore useful to discuss these motivation types in a little more detail here in order to provide a richer background for the discussions that we provide in the rest of the section. We discuss them in order of the number of responses that were found in each category, beginning with the category that received the highest number of responses: cross-modal motivations.

Cross-Modal Motivations

As we saw in Section 2, motivations that fell into the 'cross-modal' category often involved a metaphorical mapping of traits directly from the emotion to the colour, without being mediated through any kind of bodily experience. Participants often made reference to the relationship between emotional intensity and colour saturation. For example, one participant accounted for the relationship between furious and red by explaining that 'both the colour and the feeling are strong and bold'. These kinds of associations may well explain the relationship between intensity and saturation that was discussed in Section 4. Further evidence for this contention comes from the fact that participants often compared the emotion–colour associations with other similar emotion–colour correspondences. For example, one participant, who had selected a dark shade of red for the emotion 'furious' commented that they had chosen 'dark red because furious is a bit stronger and, therefore, darker than the red of anger'. A similar comment was found among the Spanish respondents (Example 1).

(1) La pasión es intensa, profunda. Es quizá un rojo granate, más que el rojo chillón, que relaciono más con el enfado. (Passion is intense, deep. It is perhaps maroon rather than bright red, which I associate with anger).

Another (British) participant who had associated excitement with orange commented in the following way (Example 2):

(2) Excited is like joy (yellow), but more anxious and maybe nervous. Orange
    has the same brightness of joy, but a brightness tempered by more ambiva-
    lent feelings of anticipation.

Interestingly, another Spanish participant referred to orange (in association with
'fearful') as inheriting properties from the personalities of yellow and red, the
two colours that orange originates from (Example 3):

(3) El naranja tiene el peligro del rojo y la crispación del amarillo. (Orange has
    the danger of red and the tension of yellow.)

Many of the responses in the cross-modal category involved a degree of
personification of the colour. For example, one American participant who had
associated passionate with the colour blue, commented that 'blue is blue and
proud'; in Spanish, another respondent chose 'ink blue' for bored because it was
'serious and boring'.

   Another American participant, who had associated passionate with purple
commented the following (Example 4):

(4) Passion runs deep and commands respect; a dark, royal purple reflects that
    depth and awe.

And another British participant who had associated excitement with orange
commented 'Bright colours scream energy'. This kind of personification was
also found in the Cantonese data. One Cantonese participant associated 'confident' with the colour brown, suggesting that 'it gives a feeling of a person being
prudent and proud'. The colour white was also found to be frequently associated
with 'confident' in the Cantonese data. For example, two Cantonese participants
explained associations with the colour white by saying that:

(5) '光明磊落,純白無瑕疵. (White is honesty and flawlessness.)

and

(6) 有自信就成個人發光. (White is the glowing light from a confident
    person.)

The way in which the emotion–colour associations were personified often
mapped the emotion's intensity onto the saturation or lightness of the colour.
In both the Spanish and the German data, for example, the emotion 'excited'
was often associated with orange, because orange was considered a 'daring',
'vibrant' and 'active' colour, thus drawing attention to the high degrees of
'intensity' of both the emotion and the colours with which it is associated.
Fearful (German 'ängstlich'), on the other hand, was associated with a rather

muted turquoise by one participant, who said that the colour, like being fearful, was 'hiding in the background' (Example 7):

(7) Ängstlich sein ist ähnlich wie schüchtern eine Farbe, die sich im Hintergrund verkriecht. (Being fearful is similar to being shy, a colour that hides in the background.)

Many of the answers in this category also contained references to valence that were then metaphorically mapped onto the associated colours. For example, one participant who had associated happiness with pink commented 'pink is a light colour and is pretty'. Likewise, when associating 'joyful' with the colour yellow, a Cantonese participant suggested that 'yellow is a bright colour and is exciting'. These kinds of associations may well explain the relationship between valence and lightness that was discussed in Section 4.

Another quality that was mapped from the emotion to the colour was complexity. For example, one American participant, who had associated happiness with purple commented that 'happiness is the combination of different things, purple is a combination of colors'. Another American participant associated jealousy with dark red, commenting 'jealous because it was bright red in its prime but now it's ageing and turning dark red until its ultimate demise of turning brown'. Similarly, a Cantonese participant explained their choice of brown for 'fearful' as a matter of complexity in that 'fearful is like many feelings mixed together and brown is a colour mixed with many different colours'.

Metaphorical thinking appears to have played a key role in the explanations that can be found in this category. In some cases, as we just saw, this took the form of personification, or at least the attribution of agency to a particular colour. In other cases, metaphorical comparisons were set up between the emotions and the colours and specific correspondences (such as the fact that both the emotion and the colour were 'complex' or 'strong'). The highly personal, almost 'poetic' nature of some of the responses in this category suggests that some colours have the ability to trigger an emotional response in humans, which is characterised by a degree of empathy, which is conducive to metaphorical thinking. For instance, an Italian participant associated 'bored' with a shade of brown (in particular, 'sand brown') and motivated this association saying that such colour is '*sciapo*', a rather informal word that can be translated as 'bland', 'unsalted' or 'lacking flavour'. In Spanish, another participant said that anger should be associated with '*rojo chillón*' (literally, 'shrieking red'). The participants in our study also attributed gender, personality as well as social and affective characteristics to the colours, which they then referred to when associating them with the emotions under consideration. The fact that this was the most common category across all languages is interesting as it suggests that the use of metaphor, and in particular personification, and the subsequent entailments that it affords is a key (and widely used) strategy for associating emotions with colours.

Environmental Motivations

The 'environmental' category was the second most popular category in our data. It included references to both the natural physical environment and the cultural environment. References to the natural physical environment mainly contained references to nature and how nature makes one feel, thus evoking a metonymic cause–effect relationship between the colour and the emotion. Respondents talked about how sunshine made them feel happy (motivating the 'happy is yellow' association), about how the sea or the ocean made them feel calm or at times sad, how grey weather made them feel depressed, and how the dark made them fearful. Responses also showed how interactions with the environment, or the absence of any interaction may motivate associations, as shown by the following response by one of our German participants for the association between 'bored' and grey (Example 8):

(8) Staub ist grau und legt sich nieder, wenn nichts passiert und keine Bewegung da ist. (Dust is grey and it forms (lit. 'comes down') when nothing happens and when there is no motion.)

Similarly, Italian participants often motivated their associations between 'bored' and grey by saying, for instance (Example 9):

(9) La noia delle giornate uggiose o nebbiose. (The boredom of dull and foggy days.)

Not surprisingly, associations between 'bored' and grey that were explained through references to nature and how nature makes one feel were also found in Cantonese (Example 10):

(10) 灰濛濛的天很悶. (Grey sky is very boring.)

Some other responses described richer references to nature, as in the case of this Spanish respondent (Example 11):

(11) El azul verdoso es una mezcla de la tranquilidad de la naturaleza y la melancolía que puede evocar un día sin sol, nublado. (Greenish blue is a mixture between the tranquillity of nature and the melancholy evoked by a cloudy sky without sun.)

References to the cultural environment were more diverse and subjective, and included comments about man-made environments such as spas, which are intended to make people feel calm and often contain white towels and white bed sheets; or to empty rooms with white walls, which were associated by an Italian participant with boredom, because 'in empty rooms there is nothing to do'. There were also references to TV shows, such as one that featured a character known as 'Mr Grey' who was meant to represent a former British Prime Minister often characterised as 'boring'. One Cantonese participant commented that 'bored is blue' because 'the life and work of the blue-collar workers are boring'. In another case, an Italian participant associated teal blue with boredom, motivating such choice with the following statement (Example 12):

(12) Il colore della copertina Bompiani del romanzo La Noia di Moravia. (The colour of the book cover by Bompiani Publishers for the novel 'La Noia' [the boredom] by Moravia.)

In some cases, cultural associations emerged that reflected how context-dependent the environmental associations could be. One of the Spanish participants associated fury with 'ruby red', not because of the strength of the feeling (as was the case with most of the responses), but because of the relationship with 'bullfighting', although it is unclear whether such relationship lies in the resemblance with the blood of the wounded bull or the colour of the bullfighter's cape.

While 'shy is pink' was not found in the top ten most frequent emotion–colour associations for any of the European languages in the study, the association ranked fourth in Cantonese (Table 9a). The fairly high ranking received by 'shy is pink' in Cantonese can possibly be explained by the fact that many Cantonese participants made reference to a man-made or culturally mediated stereotype specifically related to women and girls (Examples 13 to 16):

(13) 少female粉紅, 代表年輕所以比較改羞. (Young female is pink, meaning young and shy.)

(14) '代表female孩子的顏色, female性較容易害羞. (Meaning a female children colour, female tends to be more shy.)

(15) 比較少female的感覺. (A more young female feeling.)

(16) Pink is like a cute and pure girl. (response provided in English)

In some responses the division between the natural and the man-made environment was blurred. For example, in the German data, 'happy' was often associated with green and the motivation provided for this was the four-leaf clover, which in

German culture, as in many cultures, is a symbol for luck (given the fact that clovers usually only have three leaves and four-leaf ones are rare). Interestingly, the German participants were the only ones to mention this fact. So, while on the one hand, the motivation for the association is grounded in the natural environment, references to this particular association were culture-specific.

Bodily Based Motivations

The 'bodily based' category of motivation types was the third most popular category. It contained many metonymic references to the face (e.g. 'people turn red when they're angry'). As we will see, the majority of responses in this category referred to the colour red and either anger itself or an emotion that was similar to anger such as fury. An alternative association was offered by a Spanish participant, who associated anger with black because (Example 17):

(17) Cuando se está enfadado no se aprecian los demás colores y se ve todo negro. (When you are angry, you cannot discern the rest of colours and see everything black.)

There were occasional references to fear and its relationship with white (e.g. 'pallid face, drained of blood'), shyness and its relationship with pink (e.g. 'blushing') and associations of sadness with the colour blue (e.g. 'related to being cold and the numbness that comes with being cold'). The association of depressed with the colour black also triggered some bodily based responses; for example, 'can't see the light' in English, or a particularly vivid one in German (Example 18):

(18) Depressionen sind der schwarze Mantel, der auf den Schultern liegt und alles herunterdrueckt. (Depressions are the black cloak on your shoulders weighing everything down.)

Another bodily based motivation was provided by Italian speakers in relation to the emotion 'depressed', which was associated to the colour purple by some participants. The motivation provided was that depressed people often have dark purple shadows under their eyes. We also found in both the Spanish and the Cantonese datasets references to 'sad' as being blue, which were accompanied by the bodily based motivation that 'tears are blue'.

Linguistic Motivations

Finally, the 'linguistic' category of motivation types was the least popular of all the categories. This category contained references to linguistic expressions, usually idioms. Some of these idioms had a clear bodily basis, such as the expression 'seeing red', which refers to anger. This expression is arguably related to aforementioned bodily based associations between anger and red faces. Other responses in this category had a less clearly bodily based motivation. These included idioms such as 'green with envy' which is difficult to trace back to a bodily response – people do not turn green when they are envious (however, and by way of exception, it should be noted that some of the Spanish and German participants also associated green as well as yellow with 'jealous' because it was the colour of 'repugnant', 'rotten' and 'disgusting' things such as 'bile' or 'bowels'). Similarly, our eyes do not turn red when we are jealous of others. But interestingly there is a Cantonese idiom '眼紅' ('eye red') which is used to refer to people being in the state of jealousy.

The fact that the association between jealous and green is difficult to trace back to any clear bodily motivation also showed in the responses. In the German data, for example, many participants provided the idiom *'grün vor Neid'* – 'green with envy' – as a reason for associating 'jealous with green' while at the same time somehow being less personally convinced by the association (Examples 19 and 20):

(19) Kommt wahrscheinlich vom Ausspruch 'grün vor Neid'; Grün vor Neid, da ist die Farbauswahl durch das Sprichwort geprägt. ([The association] is probably derived from the idiom 'green with envy'; the colour choice is influenced by the idiom.)

(20) Wahrscheinlich ist Farbauswahl auch durch den vielfach gehörten Ausspruch 'grün vor Neid (sein)'geprägt. (Probably the choice of colour is influenced by the common saying '(to be) green with envy'.)

Similarly, some Italian participants motivated the association between 'jealous' and green by stating that 'it is what we are taught in language classes', 'it is an idiomatic expression' or even 'a tradition, and that is it'.

Some participants even mentioned the idiom in their response but then deliberately chose a different colour (Example 21):

(21) Auch wenn es 'Grün vor Neid' heißt, verbinde ich mit Neidisch die Farbe Rot, weil Neid innere Wut in einem auslöst. (Even if it's 'green with envy', I associate jealous with the colour red because jealous often causes an inner anger.)

This indicates that on the one hand people are aware of conventionalised cultural emotion–colour associations but that on the other hand these can be overridden by more personal, bodily based motivations, as shown in the example from the German motivation data. Associations that are motivated by references to idioms were also found in the Cantonese data. Grey was frequently associated with 'depressed', 'fearful' and 'sad', and many Cantonese participants made reference to the Cantonese idioms '好灰' (very grey) and '灰心' (grey heart), both meaning 'disappointed and frustrated', when relating emotions to grey. They also cited the Cantonese idiom '黑面' (black face), which is used to describe the colour of angry people's faces, when explaining their associations between 'furious' and black.

Idioms often have a metaphorical basis, which is accessible, on some level, to the reader or listener (Gibbs, 1993; Nayak & Gibbs, 1990). Therefore, even if the participants were not actively engaging in metaphorical thinking when they made these references to idioms, they were drawing on metaphorical ideas that have become crystallised in their languages.

5.3 How Do the Motivation Types Vary According to the Linguistic Backgrounds of the Participants?

The proportions with which the different motivation types were provided by each of the groups of participants are shown in Figure 21.

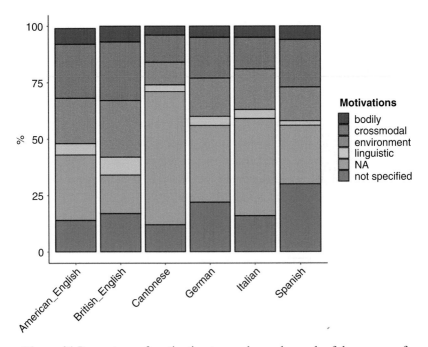

Figure 21 Percentage of motivation types chosen by each of the groups of participants

We can see from Figure 21 that the preference for different types of motiv-ations differed across the six groups of participants ($\chi^2(25) = 816.14$, p<.001). This difference in distribution, however, is mainly due to the fact that Cantonese and Italian participants exhibited particularly high numbers of cases where no response was given (NA for 'no answer') – this was the case for over half of the Cantonese participants (59%) and for almost half of the Italian participants (44%). The German and Spanish participants provided large numbers of 'unspecified' answers, with this category accounting for almost one quarter of the responses provided by the German participants and for one third of the responses provided by the Spanish participants. If we disregard these and only look at responses with either a bodily, cross-modal, environmental, or linguistic motivation, the distribution of motivation types across languages looks some-what more homogeneous (see Figure 22).

In Figure 22, we can see that the proportions for bodily based motivations are fairly evenly spread across the six different groups. The distribution is still significant ($\chi^2(15) = 60.19$, p<.001); that is, there were significant differences between the types of motivations that participants from different linguistic backgrounds provided.

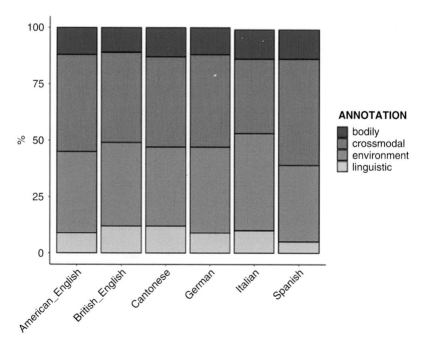

Figure 22 Percentage of motivation types chosen by each of the groups of participants (NA and unspecified answers excluded)

This difference is mainly due to an overrepresentation of cross-modal responses in the Spanish participants, environmentally based responses by Italian participants and linguistically based responses by British participants. Spanish participants were especially likely to refer to the 'personality' of the colour when motivating their associations with each feeling: the most outstanding trends were to refer to black as a 'sad' colour, brown and grey as 'boring', orange and green as 'lively and happy', pink as 'jovial and sweet', red as 'passionate', and yellow as 'happy and positive'. In turn, Italian participants often provided motivations that related to features of the natural environment (sea, mountains, snow, fog, grass, sun, etc.). They also referred to features of man-made environments. For instance, in several cases, emotion–colour associations were motivated by references to colours that are used in buildings (middle school walls are brown, so brown is associated to boredom), on book covers (publishers using specific colours on book covers) and in clothing.

5.4 How Do the Different Motivations Vary According to the Emotion Being Discussed?

Having explored the main types of motivation that were provided by participants across the board and within the different groups, we now examine the ways in which various types of motivation varied according to the emotion that was being discussed. The different motivation types were found to differ significantly in terms of the emotions with which they were associated ($\chi^2(112) = 2402.8$, p<.001). We used the residuals to identify the over-represented and under-represented emotions for each type of motivation for all groups. Results are shown in Figure 23. Green shading indicates that there is a significantly positive correlation between a motivation type and an emotion: the darker the green, the higher the residual value. Red shading indicates a negative correlation between a motivation type and an emotion.

A few interesting patterns can be observed here. First, when participants were associating colours with the emotions 'angry' and 'furious', they tended to provide bodily related explanations for their choices. As we saw in Section 3, these two emotions were strongly associated with the colour red, largely due to the fact that we experience a rush of blood to the head when we are angry. We also saw in Section 3 that these were the most frequent associations across all participants. It is also interesting to note that bodily based motivations do not appear to be provided for emotions that have high valence (e.g. cheerful, happy) or low intensity (e.g. calm, depressed). We explore this relationship in more detail later in this section. Cross-modal motivations were most likely to be associated with the emotions

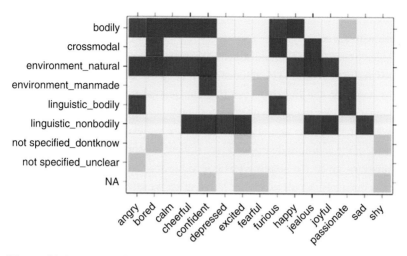

Figure 23 Summary of over-represented and under-represented associations between emotions and all motivation types (green tiles indicate attraction of associations, red tiles indicate repulsion, grey tiles indicate no significant relation).

'bored' and 'depressed'. These emotions tend to have quite low intensity ratings, suggesting that 'low-intensity' emotions are more likely to lend themselves to cross-modal associations, an idea that we will explore in more detail. Motivations relating to the natural environment were most likely to be produced when discussing the emotion 'calm' (and involved mentions of the sea or the sky), and when discussing emotions that have high valence values (cheerful and happy). These were usually associated with the colour yellow, thus activating the idea of light and sun, a relationship that was found across all languages. The natural environment was very rarely referred to when discussing more negative feelings (angry, bored, jealous) – there seemed to be a general positive perception of nature across the board. References to the cultural/man-made environment were most likely to be made when talking about the emotions 'confident' (where references were often made to the clothes one might wear) and 'passionate' (where references were made to tokens of love, such as red roses and hearts). Bodily based linguistic (idiomatic) motivations were most likely to be produced for the emotions 'angry', 'furious' and 'passionate'. All of these responses made reference to idioms relating to the bodily based associations that these emotions have with the colour red. Non-bodily linguistic motivations were most likely to be provided for the emotions 'depressed' and 'sad', which, as we saw earlier, were associated with the colour blue via a number of similar idioms in all languages. Non-bodily linguistic motivations were also associated with the emotion 'jealous', which is associated in a number of idioms with the colour green.

We have seen in the earlier discussion that motivations that made reference to the environment tended to be associated with positive emotions whereas motivations based on the linguistic environment tended to be related to negative emotions. In order to test whether this relationship was significant, and also to see whether there was any effect for intensity, we examined the valence and intensity of the emotions discussed to see if there is a connection with the type of explanations given. To obtain a numeric value for the explanations given, we took the residuals calculated earlier In doing so, we attributed more importance to the most frequent associations. Having identified the most frequent motivations that were provided by our participants when associating these emotions with colours, we then performed a Pearson correlation with the numeric values for valence/intensity for each emotion. The results from this analysis confirmed that there was a statistically significant moderate positive correlation between positive feelings and a tendency to provide environment-related motivations ($r = 0.61$, p<.05, AdjR^2 = 0.37). In other words, environmentally based motivations were more likely to be mentioned when participants were identifying colours that they associated with positive emotions. Conversely, linguistic motivations were significantly more likely to be mentioned when participants were identifying colours that they associated with negative emotions ($r = -0.67$, p<.01, AdjR^2 = 0.44). This finding chimes with previous research showing that metaphorical idioms tend to perform negative evaluative functions (Moon, 1998). There are no significant findings with respect to intensity. These findings suggest that people associate positive emotional experiences with the natural physical environment but that they are more likely to associate negative emotional experiences with idioms.

5.5 How Do the Different Motivations Vary According to the Colour Being Selected?

At this point, it is interesting to look at how the different types of motivation varied according to the colours being selected, for this set of emotions. The distribution of colours across the different motivation types was found to vary in a statistically significant way ($\chi^2(104) = 3020.1$, p<.001). Again, in order to establish whether there were any statistically significant strong or weak associations, we identified the residuals and created a summary, which is shown in Figure 24.

In Figure 24, green shading indicates that there is a significantly positive correlation between a motivation type and a colour – the darker the green, the

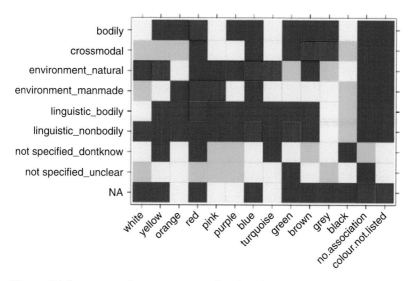

Figure 24 Summary of over-represented and under-represented associations between main colours and motivation types (green tiles indicate attraction of associations, red tiles indicate repulsion, grey tiles indicate no significant relation).

higher the residual value. Red shading indicates a negative correlation between a motivation type and a colour.

We can see here that bodily based motivations for this set of emotions were very strongly and unambiguously associated with the colour red. This can be explained by the predominance of references to the idea of 'going red in the face' in response to emotions such as anger and fury. It is also interesting to note that the 'no association' response is statistically under-represented, meaning that when people select a colour on the basis of a bodily based motivation, there is no ambiguity; people know which colour to choose.

For cross-modal motivations, we see greater variability; brown and grey were popular choices, for example. This may be explained by the fact that when participants provided a motivation of this type, they often referred to the relative properties of a colour, drawing attention to the fact that it was 'lighter/darker' or 'less/more intense' than a similar colour. One Cantonese participant reported that 'fearful' is brown (Example 22) because:

(22) 淡啡色令人感到困惑,憂心重重一樣. (Light brown makes people feel worried and anxious.)

Also associating 'fearful' with brown, another Cantonese participant provided the following comment in English:

(23) When one has many worries mixed together, it is like brown because the
colour is like many colours mixed together.

This focus on intensity is perhaps easier when the colour itself lacks hue, as
these colours do. It is interesting that 'no association' is even more strongly
avoided as an option here; participants seem to know what colours to choose
when they think there is a cross-modal motivation.

The environmentally motivated associations included numerous references to
nature and this is reflected in the colours that were chosen: yellow (sun); turquoise
(sea), blue (water, sky) and green (plants). As with associations that had bodily
based motivations, participants were also likely to avoid 'colour not listed' or 'no
association', when making environmental associations, probably because they had
clear referents in nature. Many of the motivations in this category were experiential
in that participants reported on their own interactions with nature (e.g. 'the sun
makes me feel warm'). Thus, when people make associations that are based on
their own bodily experiences, including physical interactions with the environment,
there appears to be very little ambiguity about which colour to choose. When we
look at the sub-divisions of the environmental motivations into 'natural' and 'man-
made', we see that the majority of the environmental motivations were natural. For
example, participants associated blue with emotions like 'calm' because of the sea,
which seems to induce a sense of calmness.

For the linguistically motivated associations, one of the most frequent colours
chosen was green, which was frequently motivated through references to the idiom
'green with envy', which is '*Grün for Neid*' in German, '*verde de envidia*' in
Spanish and '*verde d'invidia*' in Italian. This was followed by blue, largely due to
the idiomatic expression 'having the blues', and black, which was associated with
the idiom 'schwarz sehen' – 'to see black' (i.e. to be pessimistic about something)
in German, and the 'black dog of depression' in English. It is interesting to note that
in addition to referring to idioms in their own languages, non-English speakers
often made reference to English idioms, reflecting the status of English as an
international language. For example, one German participant selected the colour
blue for 'depressed' and provided the English phrase 'feeling blue' as a motivation.
Several Italian participants also made reference to this English idiomatic expression
and suggested that this would typically appear in songs. The Cantonese participants
also made indirect references to the English idiom 'feeling blue', for example, by
quoting 'Monday blues', 'blue Monday' and 'feeling blue' in English. This was
also the case in Spanish, where some participants associated blue with 'sad'
'because of the meaning of "blues" in English'.

When we look at the sub-divisions of the linguistic motivations comparing
those that have a bodily basis and those that do not, we see that both bodily and

non-bodily based linguistic (idiomatic) motivations tended to be used when talking about the colour black. This reflects the widespread embodied experience of it being frightening to find oneself in the dark, and the more cultural association of the colour black with depression. Non-bodily based linguistic (idiomatic) motivations were more likely to involve the colours blue and green, which largely relate to expressions, such as 'feeling blue' and 'green with envy'. The latter expression is found in other languages as well, such as in Italian, Spanish and German, as just mentioned.

For obvious reasons, when participants chose to provide no explanation, it was usually because they had not chosen a colour, either because they felt none were appropriate, or because they had wanted to select a colour that was not listed. Interestingly, this response type was rarely associated with the colours white, yellow, green, grey and black; these are the colours that for the reasons discussed are more likely to attract some kind of explanation when associated with a feeling.

It should be noted that the colour–motivation associations discussed in this section apply to this particular set of emotions and it may not be possible to generalise beyond these emotions. With this caveat in mind, we have made a number of observations here that would be worthy of further investigation. Most notably, we have seen that when people produce bodily based motivations (e.g. 'angry is red') or motivations that refer to the body's interaction with the environment (e.g. 'fearful is black'), there appears to be far more agreement and far less ambiguity than in cases where the motivations are inspired by the bodily external features or linguistic features. This may reflect the fact that bodily based experiences are more uniform across different languages and cultures. In the final part of this section, we briefly explore this issue further.

5.6 If an Association is Bodily Related, Is It More Likely to Be Widely Shared?

The final question that we aimed to address related to the extent to which the associations involving particular motivations were shared across languages and cultures. In Section 1, we hypothesised that emotion–colour associations involving mostly bodily based motivations would be more widely shared as these experiences are more likely to be widely shared.

To investigate this, we identified a subset of the emotion–colour associations that had been coded as bodily based. We then calculated the percentage of times that association received a bodily based motivation for each of the six languages and selected all cases where 50 per cent or more of the motivations were bodily based. We then ranked the associations according to the degree of agreement across the six groups of participants. We found that the emotion–colour associations that received the highest numbers of bodily based motivations, and where these motivations were most likely to be shared across the six groups, were:

- 'passionate is red', where the majority of the motivations were bodily based in the responses provided by all six groups (100 per cent of the responses provided by the British, German, Cantonese, and Italian participants'; 89 per cent of the responses provided by the American participants and 73 per cent of the responses provided by the Spanish participants)
- 'angry is red', where the majority of the motivations were bodily based in five of the groups (100 per cent in the case of the British, American and German participants, between 90 and 100 per cent in the case of the Italian, Spanish and Cantonese participants)
- 'furious is red', where the majority of the motivations were bodily based in five of the six groups (between 90 and 100 per cent in the case of the Spanish, Cantonese and German participants, and between 80 and 90 per cent in the case of the American and British participants).

These findings suggest that the most bodily based associations were especially likely to be shared across languages and cultures.

5.7 Conclusion

In our exploration of motivation types, we found a degree of convergence across the six groups of participants. In general, when a motivation type was given, the most common choice was 'cross-modal', then 'environmental', then 'bodily motivated', then 'linguistic'. However, we also found substantial variation. For example, the motivations provided by the Spanish, Italian and British participants were significantly more cross-modal, environmental and linguistic than those provided by the other participants.

We also looked at whether any of the motivations correspond closely to any of the colours or the emotions. In other words, we looked at how the emotions and the colours with which they are associated vary in terms of the motivations that they 'attract'. Interestingly, emotion–colour associations involving negative emotions (such as 'sad' or 'jealous') were most likely to be motivated by references to idioms, suggesting that metaphorical idioms are predominantly negative across all six of the linguistic/cultural groups that were investigated in this study.[15] Conversely, emotion–colour associations involving positive

---

[15] The relation between negativity and metaphoricity presents a highly interesting field for further research since the examples usually provided for conceptual metaphors often tend to be negative. For example, Lakoff and Johnson (1980) introduce the LOVE IS A JOURNEY conceptual metaphor

emotions (such as 'happy' or 'calm') were most likely to be motivated by references to the natural environment, possibly reflecting the fact that in general, the natural environment has a positive effect on people's emotions. We found that associations involving shades of red were particularly likely to involve bodily based motivation. Finally, we saw that those associations that were most likely to receive a bodily based motivation were most likely to be shared across different linguistic/cultural groups, which lends support to theories in cognitive linguistics relating to the 'universality' of embodied metaphor.

6 General Conclusions

We saw in the introduction that humans have a complex, emotional relationship with colour. We argued that by exploring this relationship in depth, looking at how it varies across languages, exploring the explanations that people provide for the associations that they make, and analysing them through the lens of metaphor, we may gain more insights into the different ways in which humans express emotions through colour, and the reasons why they do so.

To this end, we have presented findings from a large-scale investigation (with 568 participants, based in the United Kingdom, the United States, Spain, Italy, Germany and Hong Kong) in which we explored the relationship between emotions and colours in depth. We investigated the extent to which hue, saturation and lightness of a colour map onto the 'meaning', intensity and valence of an emotion, identified the reasons that people provide for these associations, and measured the extent of cross-cultural variation in the associations that are formed. Most importantly, we investigated the reasons that are offered for them. In particular, we sought to establish whether meaning, intensity and valence map neatly onto hue, saturation and lightness, and whether these relationships, and the reasons that are offered for them vary according to the linguistic background of the participants.

We have found evidence to suggest that metaphoric (and metonymic) language and thought play a key role on a number of levels in the formation of emotion–colour associations, and that, as with metaphor more generally, this takes a range of forms. We have found support for a strong metaphorical connection between the valence of the emotion and the lightness of the colours with which it is associated and between the intensity of an emotion and the saturation level of the colours with which it is associated. We have found however that the strength of this association varies according to the linguistic

---

through expressions such as 'to be at a crossroads', 'to hit rock bottom', 'to go through a difficult time', 'to go separate ways', etc.

background of the speaker, and to some extent according to the gender of the prompt.

As for the explanations that were offered for the associations, we have found that cross-modal motivations are the most common explanation, and that these draw heavily on different kinds of metaphor, including personification and the identification of vehicle-neutral mapping adjuncts (Barnden et al., 2003). Environmental motivations were also common, and these tended to involve metonymic cause–effect relationships between the colour associated with a certain environmental aspect and the emotional effect that it may have on an individual. Similarly, bodily based explanations also drew on metonymic connections between the physical effect of an emotion and the colour that it is associated with. And finally, linguistic motivations tended to draw on established metaphorical connections in the languages investigated.

These findings suggest that emotion–colour associations are shaped by a number of factors, including the ways in which we respond physically to both the natural and the man-made environment, our intrinsic responses to the colours themselves, and the linguistic environment in which we operate. These can all serve as a basis for metaphorical and metonymic connections which can take several different forms. At times, they can be highly creative and employ elements of personification, while in other cases, they draw on conventional metaphors or established conceptual mappings. All of these are susceptible to variation across languages though core relationships such as the relationships between valence and lightness and between intensity and saturation appear to operate across all the languages investigated. More positive emotions tend to be associated with lighter colours and more intense emotions tend to be associated with more saturated colours, across the board, but there are cross-cultural differences both in terms of the overall levels of lightness and saturation and in terms of the degree to which these properties are associated with one another. We have seen some evidence of an apparent 'typicality' effect with some of the colours for the cultures and languages analysed in that it tends to be a specific shade of red that is associated with angry, or furious in all languages. We have also found that typological diversity and the geographical distances between languages are somewhat reflected in the array of emotion–colour associations that are provided by their speakers, which suggest that cultural proximity also plays a role, but that there are some exceptions to this.

When we looked at the gender of the prompt, we saw that masculine adjectives exhibited a stronger relationship between valence and lightness than feminine adjectives. The strongest differences were found at the more negative end of the scale suggesting that when negative emotions are presented, they are more likely to be associated with darker colours when they appear in the masculine form than when they appear in the feminine form. No differences were found between masculine and feminine adjectives for the relationship between intensity and saturation.

Turning to the reasons that our participants offered for their choices, we have seen that, interestingly, the cross-modal associations appeared to be the most 'metaphorical' type of motivation type, involving personification and 'universal' mapping adjuncts. However, we also found substantial variation. For example, the motivations provided by the Spanish, Italian and British participants were significantly more cross-modal, environmental and linguistic than those provided by the other participants. Interestingly, we have found that emotion–colour associations involving negative emotions are most likely to be motivated by references to idioms, suggesting that metaphorical idioms are predominantly negative across all six of the linguistic/cultural groups that were investigated in this study. Conversely, emotion–colour associations involving positive emotions are most likely to be motivated by references to the natural environment, possibly reflecting the fact that in general, the natural environment has a positive effect on people's emotions. Finally, we have seen that those associations that were most likely to receive a bodily based motivation are most likely to be shared across different linguistic/cultural groups, which lends support to theories in cognitive linguistics relating to the 'universality' of embodied metaphor.

These findings suggest that our experiences with colours (in the natural world, in our cultural environments and in language) play an important role both in the ways in which we experience our own emotions and in the ways in which perceive the emotional lives of others. Colours themselves are often endowed with 'human' characteristics (e.g. 'That blue is blue and proud!') and we respond to colours in our environment in highly emotional ways, which are largely positive, with many participants commenting on how the blue of the sea or the sky makes them feel calm or that the sun makes them feel happy. In contrast, associations between negative emotions and colours are more likely to evoke 'linguistic' explanations as they are more likely to have been encoded in language through idioms. Through this study we hope to have deepened our understanding of how our experiences of emotions relate to our experiences of colour in the natural and man-made environment, and how these experiences are mediated by language, metaphor, metonymy and culture.

References

Aslam, M. M. (2006). Are you selling the right colour? A cross-cultural review of colour as a marketing cue. *Journal of Marketing Communications, 12*(1), 15–30.

Athanasopoulos, P., & Casaponsa, A. (2020). The Whorfian brain: Neuroscientific approaches to linguistic relativity. *Cognitive Neuropsychology, 37*(5–6), 393–412.

Barchard, K. A., Grob, K. E., & Roe, M. J. (2017). Is sadness blue? The problem of using figurative language for emotions on psychological tests. *Behavior Research Methods, 49*(2), 443–56.

Barnden, J. A., Glasbey, S. R., Lee, M. G., & Wallington, A. M. (2003). Domain-transcending mappings in a system for metaphorical reasoning. In *Conference companion to the 10th conference of the European chapter of the Association for Computational Linguistics* (pp. 57–61). Association for Computational Linguistics.

Barrett, L. F. (2017a). *How emotions are made: The secret life of the brain.* Houghton Mifflin Harcourt.

Barrett, L. F. (2017b). The theory of constructed emotion: An active inference account of interoception and categorization. *Social Cognitive and Affective Neuroscience, 12*(1), 1–23.

Berlin, B., & Kay, P. (1969). *Basic color terms.* University of California Press.

Bolognesi, M. (2020). *Where words get their meaning: Cognitive processing and distributional modelling of word meaning in first and second language* (vol. 23). John Benjamins.

Boroditsky, L. & Schmidt, L. A. (2000). Sex, syntax, and semantics. *Proceedings of the Annual Meeting of the Cognitive Science Society, 22.* https://escholarship.org/uc/item/0jt9w8zf.

Cannon, W. B. (1927). The James–Lange theory of emotions: A critical examination and an alternative theory. *The American Journal of Psychology, 39*(1/4), 106–24. https://doi.org/10.2307/1415404.

Chen, J., Kacinik, N. A., Chen, Y., & Wu, N. (2016). Metaphorical color representations of emotional concepts in English and Chinese speakers. Paper presented at the Annual Conference of the Cognitive Science Society, Philadelphia.

Clarke, T., & Costall, A. (2008). The emotional connotations of color: A qualitative investigation. *Color Research & Application, 33*(5), 406–10. https://doi.org/10.1002/col.20435.

Colston, H. L., & Gibbs, R. W. (2021). Figurative language communicates directly because it precisely demonstrates what we mean. *Canadian Journal of Experimental Psychology/Revue Canadienne de Psychologie Expérimentale, 75*(2), 228–33.

Cubelli, R., Paolieri, D., Lotto, L., & Job, R. (2011). The effect of grammatical gender on object categorization. *Journal of Experimental Psychology: Learning, Memory, and Cognition, 37*(2), 449–60.

Deabler, H. L. (1957). Colors and mood-tones. *Journal of Applied Psychology, 41*(5), 279–83.

Eagly, A. H., & Wood, W. (1991). Explaining sex differences in social behavior: A meta-analytic perspective. *Personality and Social Psychology Bulletin, 17*(3), 306–15. https://doi.org/10.1177/0146167291173011.

Ekman, P. (1992). An argument for basic emotions. *Cognition & Emotion, 6*(3–4), 169–200.

Fadzil, M. I., Omar, M. W., & Murad, M. H. (2011). The power of color on packaging. In IEEE (Ed.), *2011 IEEE Colloquium on Humanities, Science and Engineering* (pp. 761–4). IEEE.

Fetterman, A. K., Robinson, M. D., & Meier, B. P. (2012). Anger as 'seeing red': Evidence for a perceptual association. *Cognition & Emotion, 26*(8), 1445–58.

Forceville, C. J., & Renckens, T. (2013). The good is light and bad is dark metaphor in feature films. *Metaphor and the Social World, 3*(2), 160–79.

Fraser, T., & Banks, A. (2004). *Designer's color manual: The complete guide to color theory and application*. Chronicle Books.

Fugate, J. M. B., & Franco, C. L. (2019). What color is your anger? Assessing color-emotion pairings in English speakers. *Frontiers in Psychology, 10*, article 206.

Gibbs Jr, R. W. (1993). Why idioms are not dead metaphors. In C. Cacciari & P. Tabossi (Eds.), *Idioms: Processing, Structure, and Interpretation* (pp. 57–77). Lawrence Erlbaum.

Gilbert, A. N., Martin, R., & Kemp, S. E. (1996). Cross-modal correspondence between vision and olfaction: The color of smells. *The American Journal of Psychology, 109*, 335–51.

Goossens, L. (1990). Metaphtonymy: The interaction of metaphor and metonymy in expressions for linguistic action. *Cognitive Linguistics, 1*(3), 323–42.

Gorn, G. J., Chattopadhyay, A., Yi, T., & Dahl, D. W. (1997). Effects of color as an executional cue in advertising: They're in the shade. *Management Science, 43*(10), 1387–400.

Grady, J. (1997). Foundations of meaning: Primary metaphors and primary scenes. Doctoral dissertation, University of California. https://escholarship.org/uc/item/3g9427m2.

Grillon, C., Pellowski, M., Merikangas, K. R., & Davis, M. (1997). Darkness facilitates the acoustic startle reflex in humans. *Biological Psychiatry, 42*(6), 453–60. https://doi.org/10.1016/S0006-3223(96)00466-0.

Hanada, M. (2018). Correspondence analysis of color–emotion associations. *Color Research & Application, 43*(2), 224–37.

Heelas, P. (1996). The emotions: social, cultural and biological dimensions. In R. Harre & G. Parrot (Eds.), *The emotions: Social, cultural and biological dimensions* (pp. 171–99). Sage.

Jonauskaite, D., Abdel-Khalek, A. M., Abu-Akel, A., et al. (2019a). The sun is no fun without rain: Physical environments affect how we feel about yellow across 55 countries. *Journal of Environmental Psychology, 66*, article 101350.

Jonauskaite, D., Wicker, J., Mohr, C., et al. (2019b). A machine learning approach to quantify the specificity of colour–emotion associations and their cultural differences. *Royal Society Open Science, 6*(9), article 190741.

Jonauskaite, D., Abu-Akel, A., Dael, N., et al. (2020). Universal patterns in color–emotion associations are further shaped by linguistic and geographic proximity. *Psychological Science, 31*(10), 1245–60.

Kaya, N., & Epps, H. H. (2004). Relationship between color and emotion: A study of college students. *College Student Journal, 38*(3), 396–405.

Kehoe, E. G., Toomey, J. M., Balsters, J. H., & Bokde, A. L. (2012). Personality modulates the effects of emotional arousal and valence on brain activation. *Social Cognitive and Affective Neuroscience, 7*(7), 858–70.

Kövecses, Z. (2003). *Metaphor and emotion: Language, culture, and body in human feeling.* Cambridge University Press.

Kövecses, Z. (2005). *Metaphor in culture: Universality and variation.* Cambridge University Press.

Kövecses, Z. (2008). Metaphor and emotion. In R. W. Jr. Gibbs (Ed.), *The Cambridge handbook of metaphor and thought* (pp. 380–96). Cambridge University Press.

Krippendorff, K. (2011). Computing Krippendorff's alpha-reliability. University of Pennsylvania departmental papers.

Kuhbandner, C., & Pekrun, R. (2013). Joint effects of emotion and color on memory. *Emotion, 13*(3), 375–9.

Lakoff, G. (1993). The contemporary theory of metaphor. In A. Ortony (Ed.), *Metaphor and thought* (2nd ed.; pp. 202–51). Cambridge University Press.

Lakoff, G., & Johnson, M. (1980). *Metaphors we live by* (1st ed.). University of Chicago Press.

Lang, P. J., Greenwald, M. K., Bradley, M. M., & Hamm, A. O. (1993). Looking at pictures: Affective, facial, visceral, and behavioral reactions. *Psychophysiology, 30*(3), 261–73.

Littlemore, J. (2015). *Metonymy: Hidden shortcuts in language, thought and communication*. Cambridge University Press.

Lynn, R., & Martin, T. (1995). National differences for thirty-seven nations in extraversion, neuroticism, psychoticism and economic, demographic and other correlates. *Personality and Individual Differences, 19*(3), 403–6. https://doi.org/10.1016/0191-8869(95)00054-A.

Macnamara, J. (2019). Linguistic relativity revisited. In R. L. Cooper & B. J. Spolsky (Eds.), *The Influence of Language on Culture and Thought* (pp. 45–60). De Gruyter Mouton.

Matsuki, K. (1995). Metaphors of anger in Japanese. *Language and the Cognitive Construal of the World, 82*, 137–51.

Meier, B. P., & Robinson, M. D. (2005). The metaphorical representation of affect. *Metaphor and Symbol, 20*(4), 239–57. https://doi.org/10.1207/s15327868ms2004_1.

Meier, B. P., Robinson, M. D., Crawford, L. E., & Ahlvers, W. J. (2007). When 'light' and 'dark' thoughts become light and dark responses: Affect biases brightness judgments. *Emotion, 7*(2), 366–76.

Mikolajczuk, A. (1998). The metonymic and metaphorical conceptualisation of anger in Polish. *Speaking of Emotions: Conceptualisation and Expression, 10*, 153–91.

Montefinese, M., Ambrosini, E., Fairfield, B., & Mammarella, N. (2014). The adaptation of the Affective Norms for English Words (ANEW) for Italian. *Behavior Research Methods, 46*(3), 887–903. https://doi.org/10.3758/s13428-013-0405-3

Moon, R. (1998). *Fixed Expressions and Idioms in English: A Corpus-based Approach*. Clarendon Press.

Nayak, N. P., & Gibbs, R. W. (1990). Conceptual knowledge in the interpretation of idioms. *Journal of Experimental Psychology: General, 119*(3), 315–30.

Niemeier, S., & Dirven, R. (2000). *Evidence for linguistic relativity* (Vol. 198). John Benjamins.

Ortony, A., & Fainsilber, L. (1987). *The role of metaphors in descriptions of emotions*. Presented at the Theoretical Issues in Natural Language Processing 3.

Osgood, C. E., Suci, G. J., & Tannenbaum, P. H. (1957). *The measurement of meaning*. University of Illinois Press.

Palmer, S. E., Schloss, K. B., Xu, Z., & Prado-León, L. R. (2013). Music–color associations are mediated by emotion. *Proceedings of the National Academy of Sciences, 110*(22), 8836–41.

Pravossoudovitch, K., Cury, F., Young, S. G., & Elliot, A. J. (2014). Is red the colour of danger? Testing an implicit red–danger association. *Ergonomics, 57*(4), 503–10.

Pütz, M., & Verspoor, M. (2000). *Explorations in linguistic relativity* (vol. 199). Amsterdam: John Benjamins.

Reisenzein, R. (1994). Pleasure-arousal theory and the intensity of emotions. *Journal of Personality and Social Psychology, 67*(3), 525–39.

Ruiz De Mendoza Ibáñez, F. J. & Díez Velasco, O. I. (2002). Patterns of conceptual interaction. In Ralf Pörings & René Dirven (Eds.), *Metaphor and metonymy in comparison and contrast* (pp. 489–532). De Gruyter.

Ruiz de Mendoza Ibáñez, F. J. & Galera Masegosa, A. (2011). Going beyond metaphtonymy: Metaphoric and metonymic complexes in phrasal verb interpretation. *Language Value*, 3, 1–29.

Russell, J. A., & Barrett, L. F. (1999). Core affect, prototypical emotional episodes, and other things called emotion: Dissecting the elephant. *Journal of Personality and Social Psychology, 76*(5), 805–19.

Sandford, J. (2021). *The sense of color: A cognitive linguistic analysis of color words*. Aguaplano.

Sandford, J. L. (2014). Turn a colour with emotion: A linguistic construction of colour in English. *JAIC-Journal of the International Colour Association, 13*, 67–83.

Sapir, E. (1929). The status of linguistics as a science. *Language*, 5(1), 207–14.

Sato, S., & Athanasopoulos, P. (2018). Grammatical gender affects gender perception: Evidence for the structural-feedback hypothesis. *Cognition, 176*, 220–31.

Schachter, S., & Singer, J. (1962). Cognitive, social, and physiological determinants of emotional state. *Psychological Review, 69*(5), 379–99.

Schifferstein, H. N., & Tanudjaja, I. (2004). Visualising fragrances through colours: The mediating role of emotions. *Perception, 33*(10), 1249–66.

Slobin, D. I. (1996). From 'thought and language' to 'thinking for speaking'. In S. Gumperz and S. Levinson (Eds.), *Rethinking linguistic relativity* (pp. 70–96). Cambridge University Press.

Slobodenyuk, N., Jraissati, Y., Kanso, A., Ghanem, L., & Elhajj, I. (2015). Cross-Modal Associations between Color and Haptics. *Attention, Perception, & Psychophysics, 77*(4), 1379–95. https://doi.org/10.3758/s13414-015-0837-1

Soriano, C., & Valenzuela, J. (2009). Emotion and colour across languages: Implicit associations in Spanish colour terms. *Social Science Information, 48* (3), 421–45. https://doi.org/10.1177/0539018409106199.

Spence, C., Levitan, C., Shankar, M., & Zampini, M. (2010). Does food color influence taste and flavor perception in humans? *Chemosensory Perception, 3*(1), 68–84.

Sutton, T. M., & Altarriba, J. (2016). Color associations to emotion and emotion-laden words: A collection of norms for stimulus construction and selection. *Behavior Research Methods*, *48*(2), 686–728.

Waggoner, J. E., & Palermo, D. S. (1989). Betty is a bouncing bubble: Children's comprehension of emotion-descriptive metaphors. *Developmental Psychology*, *25*(1), 152–63.

Wahl, S., Engelhardt, M., Schaupp, P., Lappe, C., & Ivanov, I. V. (2019). The inner clock: Blue light sets the human rhythm. *Journal of Biophotonics*, *12* (12), article e201900102. https://doi.org/10.1002/jbio.201900102.

Walters, J., Apter, M. J., & Svebak, S. (1982). Color preference, arousal, and the theory of psychological reversals. *Motivation and Emotion*, *6*(3), 193–215.

Wang, T., Shu, S., & Mo, L. (2014). Blue or red? The effects of colour on the emotions of C hinese people. *Asian Journal of Social Psychology*, *17*(2), 152–8.

Warriner, A. B., Kuperman, V., & Brysbaert, M. (2013). Norms of valence, arousal, and dominance for 13,915 English lemmas. *Behavior Research Methods*, *45*(4), 1191–207. https://doi.org/10.3758/s13428-012-0314-x.

Wee, Y. C., & Gopalakrishnakone, P. (1990). *A colour guide to dangerous plants*. NUS Press.

Wexner, L. B. (1954). The degree to which colors (hues) are associated with mood-tones. *Journal of Applied Psychology*, *38*(6), 432–5.

Whorf, B. L. (1940). *Science and linguistics*. Bobbs-Merrill.

Winawer, J., Witthoft, N., Frank, M. C., Wu, L., Wade, A. R., & Boroditsky, L. (2007). Russian blues reveal effects of language on color discrimination. *Proceedings of the National Academy of Sciences*, *104*(19), 7780–5.

Acknowledgements

We are grateful to all our 568 participants from the United Kingdom, the United States, Spain, German, Italy and Hong Kong for having made this study possible. We would like to thank Meryem Clarke for her insightful comments on possible sources of emotion–colour correspondences, and Olivia Haysman-Walker for her assistance with coding the data. Special thanks go to Bodo Winter for very generously sharing his 'theme_bham_stats' package, which allows for the production of elegant plots in R. Finally, we are indebted to the editors of this Cambridge Elements series, Sarah Duffy and Nick Riches, and the two anonymous reviewers, for their support and valuable feedback on earlier versions of this manuscript. The present study has been funded in part by the State Agency of Research – Spanish Ministry of Science, Innovation and Universities (FFI2017-82730-P, PID2020-118349GB-I00 and PID2021-123302NB-I00) and by the University of Birmingham Research and Knowledge Transfer Fund.

For Nora, Gereon and Angela, the newest members of the team!

Cambridge Elements ≡

Cognitive Linguistics

Sarah Duffy
Northumbria University
Sarah Duffy is Senior Lecturer in English Language and Linguistics at Northumbria University. She has published primarily on metaphor interpretation and understanding, and her forthcoming monograph for Cambridge University Press (co-authored with Michele Feist) explores *Time, Metaphor, and Language* from a cognitive science perspective. Sarah is Review Editor of the journal, *Language and Cognition*, and Vice President of the UK Cognitive Linguistics Association.

Nick Riches
Newcastle University
Nick Riches is a Senior Lecturer in Speech and Language Pathology at Newcastle University. His work has investigated language and cognitive processes in children and adolescents with autism and developmental language disorders, and he is particularly interested in usage-based accounts of these populations.

Editorial Board
Heng Li, *Southwest University*
John Newman, *University of Alberta (Edmonton)*
Kimberley Pager-McClymont, *University of Huddersfield*
Katie J. Patterson, *Universidad de Granada*
Maria Angeles Ruiz-Moneva, *University of Zaragoza*
Lexi Webster, *Manchester Metropolitan University*
Xu Wen, *Southwest University*

About the Series
Cambridge Elements in Cognitive Linguistics aims to extend the theoretical and methodological boundaries of cognitive linguistics. It will advance and develop established areas of research in the discipline, as well as address areas where it has not traditionally been explored and areas where it has yet to become well established.

Cambridge Elements ≡

Cognitive Linguistics

Printed in the United States
by Baker & Taylor Publisher Services